GREAT MEALS
with GREENS
and GRAINS

OVER **80** RECIPES FOR DELICIOUS
and HEALTHY VEGETARIAN DISHES

MEGAN WOLF, MS, RD

FOUNDER OF MEGAN WOLF NUTRITION LLC AND
THE FOOD BLOG THE DOMESTICATED WOLF

PAGE STREET
PUBLISHING CO.

PAGE STREET
PUBLISHING CO.

First published in 2016 by

Page Street Publishing Co.

27 Congress Street, Suite 103

Salem, MA 01970

www.pagestreetpublishing.com

Distributed by Macmillan, sales in Canada by The Canadian Manda Group.

19 18 17 16   1 2 3 4 5

ISBN-13: 978-1-62414-228-4

ISBN-10: 1-62414-228-1

Library of Congress Control Number: 2015912873

Cover and book design by Page Street Publishing Co.

Photography by Megan Wolf

Printed and bound in China

Page Street is proud to be a member of 1% for the Planet. Members donate one percent of their sales to one or more of the over 1,500 environmental and sustainability charities across the globe who participate in this program.

TO MY MOTHER, SELMA, WHO TAUGHT ME EVERYTHING
I KNOW ABOUT THE KITCHEN AND BEYOND.

CONTENTS

DARK LEAFY GREENS · 47

APPETIZERS

Wilted Greens and Sautéed Mushroom Crostini · 48

Mustard Green and White Bean Hummus with Spiced Pita Chips · 51

SALADS

Kale Salad with Candied Almonds, Apples and Maple Dressing · 52

Kale Caesar with Challah Croutons · 55

Farmers' Market Kale Salad with Apples and Radish · 56

SOUPS

Rustic Kale Pesto Soup with Zucchini and White Beans · 59

ENTRÉES

Rainbow Chard and Parmesan Quiche · 60

Lacinato Kale and Caramelized Onion Galette · 62

Baked Eggs with Feta and Kale · 63

Moo Shu Vegetables in Collard Green Wraps · 64

Crispy Tofu Collard Green Tacos with Peanut Sauce · 65

Sun-Dried Tomato Ricotta Rigatoni with Kale and White Wine · 67

SIDE DISHES

Green Goddess Kale, Two Ways · 68

OTHER GREEN GOODIES · 71

APPETIZERS

Green Heirloom Tomatoes with Mozzarella and Nectarines · 72

Asparagus and Egg Puff Pastry · 75

SALADS

Cool Cucumber Salad with Dill and Red Onion · 76

Roasted Zucchini Salad with Feta and White Beans · 77

Spicy Broccoli Salad · 78

Very Green Israeli Salad · 79

SOUPS

Chilled Pea Soup with Mint and Greek Yogurt · 80

Broccoli and Parmesan Soup · 83

ENTRÉES
Seared Thai Eggplant Naan with Tzatziki · 84

Perciatelli with Broccoli Rabe and Roasted Garlic Cream Sauce · 87

Asparagus Galette with Lemon and Parmesan · 88

SIDE DISHES
Double Chocolate Zucchini Muffins · 90

Toasted Pumpkin Seed, Cucumber and Avocado Salad · 91

Tangy Green Bean and Potato Salad · 91

ANCIENT GRAINS · 93

APPETIZERS
Quinoa and Kale Falafel · 94

SALADS
Quinoa Salad with Mint, Zucchini Chips and Walnuts · 97

Wheat Berries with Sautéed Mushrooms and Garlic Scape Pesto · 98

Summer Corn Pesto Salad with Wheat Berries and Arugula · 99

Barley Salad with Roasted Green Beans, Radish and Hazelnuts · 100

Farro Salad with Roasted Sweet Potatoes, Brussels Sprouts and Hazelnuts · 101

Lemon Herb Barley Salad with Fava Beans · 102

SOUPS
Winter Farro Vegetable Soup · 105

ENTRÉES
Toasted Wheat Berries with White Beans, Burst Tomatoes and Parmesan · 106

Crunchy Quinoa, Goat Cheese and Pistachio–Stuffed Acorn Squash · 109

Marsala Mushroom Farro Risotto · 110

Spice-Rubbed Eggplant with Quinoa and Cherries · 113

Veggie Burgers with Farro, Cumin and Honey Mustard · 114

Freekeh Grain Bowl with Walnut Vinaigrette and a Poached Egg · 116

Eggplant Quinoa Meatballs · 117

Smoky BBQ Tofu Salad Grain Bowl with Kaniwa · 119

SIDE DISHES
Wheat Berry Salad with Mint and Cranberries · 120

Blackberry Quinoa Scones with Maple Glaze · 121

Pumpkin Cranberry Amaranth Muffins · 122

INTRODUCTION

This book is meant for people who love to cook and love to eat. It focuses on greens and grains—two of the healthiest foods available, rich in vitamins, minerals, fiber and nutrients our bodies need on a daily basis. While these foods are incredibly healthy, that's not to say their flavors cannot be enhanced with the help of something really delicious. What's a world without cheese, nuts, flavorful oils, seasonings and spices?

My blog, The Domesticated Wolf, started because friends would constantly ask me for recipes and it seemed more efficient to post online instead of emailing or texting ingredients and directions (and answering questions along the way). As my nutrition practice grew, clients too would ask for recipes. I hope this book serves to inspire family, friends, clients and home cooks to broaden their palates, explore different flavors and incorporate more greens and grains into their daily diets.

I've quite literally always loved greens—even before they were fashionable. My father still tells a story about taking my friends and me bowling at the tender age of five. As my friends and I sidled up to the snack bar, my father indulged us and said that we could order anything we wanted. While girl after girl ordered pizza, nachos and French fries, I patiently waited my turn, and when the server turned to me, I ever so politely asked, "May I please have the salad?" Fast-forward twenty-five years, and not much has changed. I may be a new mother, and my feet may now reach the ground when I sit on a barstool, but I'm still loving greens, and how lucky am I that I get to author my first book focused on them?

Through my work as a registered dietitian, I aim to inspire my clients and instill in them a love for healthy eating. But to many, leafy green vegetables are bland, unexciting, something your mother made you eat as a child and, dare I say, "rabbit food." The reality is, Mom was right! Greens are not only nutrient powerhouses, rich in so many vital vitamins, but they are also perfect canvases for so many flavors. If you can start with a healthy base—maybe kale, arugula or mixed greens—and layer your favorite flavors atop, you are in for a treat.

And don't even get me started on grains. They run the gamut from the familiar to those less so, are incredibly versatile, chock-full of satisfying fiber and nutrients, and they keep you full and happy. By learning how to use them, and mixing and matching, you can create a veritable unlimited supply of recipes.

That is what I find so exciting! Cooking, to me, is not about rigid rules that demand strict adherence to a recipe "or else." The kitchen should be a bright, vibrant place where you can be creative and feel unintimidated.

These recipes should be a guideline to demystify the experience and allow you to customize meals to your tastes. The astute reader may notice that not a single recipe contains black pepper. Why? Because I don't particularly enjoy it. And I hope that you enjoy this same malleability when tailoring recipes to your palate. Prefer a bit of a kick? Add red pepper flakes or a dash of Tabasco, Sriracha or your favorite hot sauce. These recipes should be your guide and inspiration, not your Bible. By making them your own, they will fast become family favorites.

I hope that you love these recipes, and that they will wow your family and friends like they have mine. But even more so, I hope that they inspire you to create new and exciting combinations for you and your loved ones. It is my sincere hope that the inspiration you glean from this book affords you untold fun creating, enjoying and sharing new food memories.

LIGHT LEAFY GREENS

Light leafy greens are similarly healthy to dark leafy greens but are not only lighter in color, but often lighter in texture, too. Think of them as the delicate younger sister to dark leafy greens.

Light leafy greens are versatile enough to drive the dish as a prominent ingredient or take a backseat role to brighten the dish and add complexity and nutrition. My Charred Mexican Street Corn Salad (page 17) highlights peppery arugula to balance the sweetness of the corn and salty bite of the cheese for a delicious main course. Alternatively, the Oven-Crisped Potatoes with Spinach Chimichurri (page 40) utilize spinach in a nontraditional way to create a tangy, pungent accompaniment to the crispy, creamy potatoes.

SAUTÉED SPINACH, FETA AND ZA'ATAR PUFF PASTRY

Za'atar is a delicious, earthy and savory spice used in many Middle Eastern dishes. I grew up eating za'atar, thanks to my mom's love for Middle Eastern food, and now it's one of my favorite flavors. Za'atar is easy to find in many Middle Eastern grocers or in upscale food markets with extensive spice sections. This recipe works well as an appetizer or side dish, and is simple to double for a larger crowd.

SERVES 4

1 sheet all-butter puff pastry

2 tbsp (30 ml) olive oil, divided

5 oz (142 g) baby spinach

1 clove garlic, minced

Juice of ½ lemon

¼ cup (38 g) crumbled feta cheese

1 tbsp (16 g) za'atar

1 egg, beaten

Salt to taste

Thaw the puff pastry for 30 to 40 minutes, or until the dough is cold but pliable. Unfold the dough and immediately place it on a greased, nonstick baking sheet or parchment paper–lined baking sheet.

Preheat the oven to 350°F (180°C).

Heat 1 tablespoon (15 ml) of the olive oil in a skillet. Once the oil is hot, add the spinach and garlic, stirring often. Cook until wilted, about 3 minutes.

Run the tip of a paring knife along the edge of the dough to form a 1-inch (2.5-cm) border. Don't cut all the way through; just score the dough as if you were making a picture frame in the pastry. Top the dough with the sautéed spinach, lemon juice, feta and za'atar. Be sure to stay inside the lines of the pastry, as if inserting a picture within the inner frame. As the pastry cooks, the outer rim will rise and form a crust around the filling.

Drizzle the remaining 1 tablespoon (15 ml) olive oil over the top, then brush the crust with the beaten egg and bake until golden brown and puffed, about 30 minutes.

Sprinkle with salt as soon as it comes out of the oven, then slice into squares or rectangles with a knife or pizza cutter.

TIPS: I have never made puff pastry—it's so easy (and just as delicious!) to buy it frozen. Save yourself serious time by purchasing it.

This dish is best served fresh out of the oven. It's perfect to pop into the oven as soon as guests arrive.

LENTIL LETTUCE WRAPS WITH CILANTRO–LIME RICE

Lentils are not only packed with protein and fiber, but they are also so meaty! Like mushrooms, they can easily take the place of meat in many dishes. These lettuce wraps are inspired by traditional Asian-style chicken lettuce wraps, but are vegetarian and so delicious. When I was pregnant with our daughter, I craved spicy foods. Although I was never a spice lover prior to getting pregnant, these spicy lentil lettuce wraps satisfy my craving and my desire for delicious home-cooked meals.

SERVES 4

SAUCE

3 tbsp (45 ml) hoisin sauce

2 tbsp (30 ml) Sriracha sauce, plus more for topping

2 tbsp (30 ml) lime juice

1 tsp soy sauce

1 tsp brown sugar (optional)

LETTUCE WRAPS

1 cup (198 g) French lentils

3 cups (720 ml) water, divided

2 pinches salt, divided

½ cup (93 g) white rice

2 cloves garlic, minced

2" (5-cm) piece of ginger, minced

1 tbsp (15 ml) sesame oil

2 tbsp (30 ml) lime juice

½ cup (8 g) chopped cilantro, divided

1 head Boston or Bibb lettuce, leaves separated

½ cup (69 g) toasted and shelled peanuts

1 jalapeño, very thinly sliced

To make the sauce: Combine all of the sauce ingredients in a small bowl and set aside.

To make the lettuce wraps: Combine the lentils, 2 cups (480 ml) of the water and a pinch of the salt in a pot and bring to a boil. Cover the pot, reduce the heat to low and cook for 30 minutes, or until the lentils are soft; drain and set aside.

While the lentils cook, in another pot, combine the rice, remaining 1 cup (240 ml) water and remaining pinch of salt and bring to a boil. Cover, reduce the heat to low and cook for 10 minutes, then turn the heat off and let the rice steam, covered, with the residual heat for 10 minutes. All of the liquid should be absorbed by the end of cooking.

In a skillet, sauté the garlic and ginger in the sesame oil until soft and fragrant, about 3 minutes.

Add the cooked lentils and reserved sauce to the garlic and ginger and stir to combine. Add the lime juice and half of the chopped cilantro to the rice, and stir to combine.

Plate each component separately or assemble individual lettuce wraps by taking one lettuce leaf and layering the rice, lentils, peanuts, remaining cilantro and jalapeño slices. Drizzle with additional Sriracha sauce, if desired.

SPICY SPINACH RICOTTA TOASTS WITH HONEY

Toast is in! I mean, really, when was toast ever "out"? Maybe during the low-carb diet craze. But it is so good and especially popular right now. This is a perfect party food: easy to make, quick to assemble and beyond delicious with its sweet, savory and spicy notes.

SERVES 4

---

1 tbsp (15 ml) olive oil

4 cups (120 g) baby spinach, rinsed and dried

4 slices whole-grain bread

¾ cup (186 g) ricotta cheese

2 tbsp (30 ml) honey

1 tsp red pepper flakes

½ tsp salt

Heat the olive oil in a large skillet over medium heat and sauté the spinach until wilted, about 3 minutes, then set aside.

Toast each slice of bread until golden brown.

Evenly spread the ricotta over each piece of toast. Top each toast with sautéed spinach, drizzle with the honey and then garnish with the red pepper flakes and salt. Serve immediately.

*See photo on page 10.

TIPS: You may wish to forgo measuring the honey and just drizzle it right over the top of each toast.

Using a flaky salt such as Maldon produces a beautiful finished product and a deliciously savory crunch with each bite.

CHARRED MEXICAN STREET CORN SALAD

Whenever I'm at a Mexican restaurant, I love to order Mexican street corn. I'm always drawn to the crunchy bite of the corn paired with the creamy and tangy cotija cheese. But, I really do not enjoy the taste of mayonnaise with lime juice, cheese and corn. In this recipe, I swap the mayonnaise for Greek yogurt, which gives the chipotle dressing a velvety texture without the heaviness or sweetness of mayonnaise. I also serve the salad with arugula, which holds up really nicely against the smoky, spicy flavors of the salad. Black beans round out my nontraditional take on a classic Mexican dish.

SERVES 4

CHIPOTLE DRESSING

2 chipotle peppers in adobo sauce

¼ cup (60 ml) adobo sauce (from canned chipotle)

¼ cup (60 g) low-fat Greek yogurt

1 tbsp (15 ml) olive oil

¼ cup (60 ml) lime juice, plus more for serving

Salt to taste

SALAD

1 cup (141 g) cooked corn kernels

2 tsp (10 ml) olive oil

10 oz (288 g) arugula

1 cup (240 g) canned black beans, rinsed and drained

4 scallions, thinly sliced

Salt to taste

2 tbsp (2 g) chopped cilantro

¼ cup (30 g) grated cotija cheese

To make the dressing: Add the dressing ingredients to a blender or food processor and combine until well incorporated. Season to taste with salt and set aside.

To make the salad: In a cast-iron pan, toss the corn kernels in olive oil and char over high heat, about 4 minutes. Set aside.

In a large bowl, combine the arugula, black beans, scallions and cooled charred corn. Toss with the chipotle dressing and season to taste with salt.

Garnish with the cilantro and cotija cheese, and serve immediately with extra lime juice on the side.

TIP: Fresh or frozen corn works great in this recipe. Canned corn is often unnecessarily salty, and lacks the freshness of the other two options.

SPINACH SALAD WITH QUINOA, TOASTED PISTACHIOS AND CRANBERRIES

My husband is not a fan of olives, so this salad is reserved for nights I'm cooking for just one, or for when I host a weekend girls' brunch. The colors are bright and vibrant and the flavors stand up on their own, but also pair nicely with other dishes. Cerignola olives are plump and buttery and impart such a lovely, subtle briny flavor to the dish. Cooking isn't about making yourself crazy searching high and low for obscure ingredients! So, if you can't find the Cerignola variety, use what you love and can easily locate.

SERVES 4

LEMON VINAIGRETTE

¼ cup (60 ml) olive oil

Juice of 1 lemon

2 cloves garlic, pushed through a garlic press or very well minced

¼ tsp salt (or more to your taste)

SALAD

¼ cup (43 g) quinoa

1 cup (240 ml) water

½ cup (69 g) shelled pistachios

10 oz (280 g) baby spinach

1 medium Anjou pear

½ cup (61 g) dried sweetened cranberries

½ cup (67 g) pitted and sliced Cerignola olives

Salt to taste

To make the lemon vinaigrette: Whisk all of the ingredients together.

To make the salad: Combine the quinoa and water in a pot and bring to a boil. Once the water is boiling, turn down the heat to low, cover the pot and cook another 10 minutes, or until the quinoa has softened and the water has evaporated; set aside.

Toast the pistachios in a small skillet over low heat until they are just golden brown and fragrant, 3 to 5 minutes; set aside.

Place the spinach in a large bowl. Thinly slice the pear and add it to the bowl along with the cranberries and olives.

Just prior to serving, add the toasted pistachios and cooked quinoa, toss with the lemon vinaigrette and season to taste with salt.

Serve family style or in individual bowls or on plates.

TIP: Getting the garlic really finely minced or crushed will help the flavor dissipate so that instead of biting into a piece of raw garlic, the salad is nicely seasoned with a garlic essence.

CRISPY LETTUCE SALAD
WITH CHICKPEAS, FETA AND DILL VINAIGRETTE

I'm a Greek cuisine fanatic. Truly, it might be my favorite cuisine, which says a lot because I (really!) love food. In New York City, we have some amazing Greek restaurants, with menus packed with olives, dill and feta cheese. This salad, inspired by my favorite Greek dishes, is crunchy and satisfying, yet incredibly light.

SERVES 4

DRESSING

½ cup (120 ml) olive oil

¼ cup (60 ml) red wine vinegar

2 tbsp (1 g) minced fresh dill, plus more for garnish

4 cloves garlic, roughly chopped

½ tsp salt

SALAD

1 head iceberg lettuce

1 can (15 oz [420 g]) chickpeas, drained and rinsed

1 cup (149 g) sliced cherry tomatoes

1 cup (92 g) sliced yellow bell pepper

½ cup (58 g) thinly sliced red onion

½ cup (75 g) crumbled feta cheese

To make the dressing: Add all the ingredients to a blender or food processor. Combine very well, and season to taste with more salt if needed. Set aside.

To make the salad: Slice the lettuce into bite-size pieces. In a large bowl, combine the lettuce, chickpeas, cherry tomatoes, pepper, red onion and feta cheese. Toss gently with half of the salad dressing, adding extra if you like a more heavily dressed salad.

Garnish with additional dill and serve family style or on individual plates.

TIPS: Acidic flavors such as red wine vinegar often mimic salty flavors, so you may not need extra salt. But always cater to your tastes, seasoning as you cook—or in this case, assemble.

This salad will keep for a few hours, but the red wine vinegar will begin to alter the texture of the vegetables. I prefer serving (and eating!) this salad immediately after making it.

RED LETTUCE GARDEN SALAD WITH CRISPY VEGETABLES

I have a childhood friend who lives just outside of New York City. She has a beautiful house, a big backyard and the loveliest garden. Although it's close to where my husband and I live, it feels like miles away! I'm often the lucky recipient of her handpicked goodies, including the sweetest red leaf lettuces. If you ever have the opportunity to sample true garden lettuce, you will not be disappointed!

SERVES 4

DRESSING

2 tbsp (30 ml) balsamic vinegar

1 tsp honey mustard

¼ cup (60 ml) olive oil

Salt to taste

SALAD

4 cups (228 g) red lettuce leaves, rinsed and dried

2 mini seedless cucumbers, sliced

2 radishes, sliced or quartered

½ cup (75 g) sliced cherry tomatoes

¼ cup (28 g) toasted chopped pecans

1 avocado, peeled, pitted and diced

¼ cup (30 g) dried cranberries (optional)

To make the dressing: Whisk together the vinegar and mustard in a bowl until thick. Drizzle in the olive oil and whisk until incorporated. Season to taste with salt and set aside.

To make the salad: In a large bowl, toss the lettuce with half of the dressing, then add the cucumbers, radishes, cherry tomatoes and toasted pecans. Add the remaining dressing and toss to combine again. Top the salad with the diced avocado and dried cranberries, if desired, and serve immediately.

TIPS: If you are using garden fresh lettuce, be sure to rinse the leaves very well—they will contain much more dirt than the lettuce at the grocery store!

If you're looking for a bit more sweetness in your salad, top it with dried cranberries or your favorite dried fruit.

WARM ESCAROLE SALAD
WITH APPLES AND HAZELNUTS

Who said salads have to be served cold? This salad contrasts warm greens, crisp apples and crunchy hazelnuts for a sublime marriage. Escarole is a mildly bitter green, so the sweet vinaigrette and apples balance the dish perfectly. I like to leave the skins on both the apples and the hazelnuts in this recipe—more color, more texture and more fiber!

SERVES 4

VINAIGRETTE

¼ cup (60 ml) olive oil

¼ cup (60 ml) apple cider vinegar

2 tbsp (30 ml) honey mustard

Salt to taste

SALAD

2 tsp (10 ml) olive oil

2 heads escarole, roughly chopped

¼ cup (34 g) chopped hazelnuts

2 medium crisp and tart apples such as Granny Smith, Fuji or Jazz varieties, cored and thinly sliced

To make the vinaigrette: Combine all the ingredients together in a bowl and whisk well. Set aside.

To make the salad: Heat the olive oil in a skillet over medium-low heat. Once the oil is hot, add the escarole and cook, covered, until the greens are just wilted, 1 to 2 minutes.

While the escarole is cooking, heat another skillet over low heat. Add the chopped hazelnuts and heat through until warm and fragrant, about 2 minutes.

In a large bowl, combine the sautéed escarole with the sliced apples, toasted nuts and vinaigrette. Serve immediately.

TIPS: An easy way to dress a salad or vegetable dish is to pour your dressing into the bottom of your serving bowl and then pile the ingredients on top. Toss to coat. Make sure you are using a large bowl so you have enough space to work. Then run a clean dishtowel or paper towel around the edge of the dish to clean up any spills or splatters.

Toasting nuts and spices releases their essential oils and is a great way to coax more flavor out of your dishes without adding salt or other ingredients.

CREAMY WHITE BEAN SOUP WITH SAUTÉED SPINACH

My mom and I are really similar—such a compliment for me! Included in our shared interests are coffee and soup, and she is famous for her lattes. I look forward to these warm, culinary hugs, often served in huge white ceramic mugs. This soup reminds me of her, so I've been serving it in the same white ceramic mugs she serves her lattes in.

SERVES 4

1 head garlic, top quarter sliced off and discarded

¼ cup (60 ml) olive oil, divided, plus more for garnish

1 tbsp (14 g) butter

1 medium Vidalia onion, sliced

2 ½ cups (590 ml) low-sodium vegetable stock, divided

1 dried bay leaf

2 cans (15 oz [420 g] each) white beans, rinsed and drained, divided

½ cup (50 g) shredded Parmesan cheese

Salt to taste

5 oz (140 g) baby spinach

Preheat the oven to 375°F (190°C).

Place the garlic on a piece of aluminum foil and drizzle with 1 tablespoon (15 ml) of the olive oil. Wrap into a pouch and roast for 30 to 40 minutes, or until the garlic is soft and golden brown.

In a large stockpot, heat 2 tablespoons (30 ml) of the olive oil and the butter over medium heat. Add the onion and cook until soft, stirring occasionally, about 5 minutes.

Add 2 ¼ cups (530 ml) of the vegetable stock, the bay leaf and 1 can of the white beans to the onions. Bring the mixture to a boil, then reduce the heat to low and let simmer for about 20 minutes.

Once the garlic is roasted, add it to the soup by popping each clove out of its protective paper. In batches, transfer to a blender or food processor and purée until smooth, then pour the soup back into the stockpot.

Add the remaining can of white beans, remaining ¼ cup (60 ml) cup vegetable stock and the Parmesan to the puréed mixture and heat through, about 10 minutes. Season to taste with salt.

In a sauté pan, heat the remaining 1 tablespoon (15 ml) olive oil, then add the spinach. Cook until completely wilted, about 4 minutes.

To serve, pour equal amounts of the soup into each of 4 bowls and top with the sautéed spinach and an extra drizzle of olive oil.

TIPS: Make sure you are constantly scraping the bottom of the stockpot—that's where so much flavor lives!

Use the best olive oil you can find; it really makes such a difference, especially when used as a garnish.

SPINACH PIZZA WITH MOZZARELLA AND HERBED RICOTTA

Homemade pizza is so fun to prepare and really quite easy. Once you have the dough making part down, the rest of the recipe is as easy as can be. This pizza is packed with creamy flavor from the mozzarella and ricotta but is nicely balanced by the hearty fresh herbs and cooked spinach. My dad taught me a trick for reheating pizza: always use cornmeal on your baking sheet or pizza stone. I've followed his lead ever since and this recipe is no exception.

SERVES 4

PIZZA DOUGH

1 cup plus 1 tbsp (255 ml) water

1 packet (2 ¼ tsp [8 g]) active dry yeast

1 tbsp (15 g) brown sugar

3 tbsp (45 ml) olive oil, divided

2 ¾ cups (330 g) all-purpose flour, and more for rolling out dough

1 tsp salt

GREENS

5 oz (144 g) baby spinach, rinsed and dried

1 tbsp (15 ml) olive oil

2 cloves garlic, minced

RICOTTA MIXTURE

1 cup (248 g) ricotta cheese

1 cup (24 g) basil leaves

Pinch of salt

Drizzle of olive oil

¼ cup (30 g) cornmeal

8 oz (225 g) mozzarella cheese, sliced

2 medium tomatoes on the vine, sliced

Salt to taste

Red pepper flakes (optional)

To make the dough: In the bowl of a stand mixer fitted with a dough hook, mix the water, yeast, brown sugar and 2 tablespoons (30 ml) of the olive oil until well combined. Let sit for about 5 minutes.

Add 2 ¾ cups (330 g) of the flour and the salt to the yeast mixture, turn the stand mixer on low and work into a ball.

Grease a large bowl with the remaining 1 tablespoon (15 ml) olive oil. Once the dough has formed, remove it from the mixing bowl and knead it with your hands for 1 minute. Place the dough in the greased bowl and coat all sides with olive oil by flipping it over a few times. Cover the bowl and place it in a warm part of your kitchen for 1 hour.

While the dough rises, make the greens: In a skillet over medium heat, sauté the spinach in the olive oil and garlic until wilted. Roughly chop and then squeeze out any liquid and set aside.

Preheat the oven to 425°F (220°C).

To make the ricotta mixture: In a blender, combine the ricotta and basil until both are well incorporated and the mixture turns green. Add the salt and mix again.

After the dough has risen for an hour, deflate it by punching it down. Flour a large cutting board, counter or a marble baking slab with the additional flour and begin to form the dough into your pizza shape.

Coat a large baking sheet with a drizzle of olive oil and the cornmeal.

Transfer the stretched dough to the baking sheet and re-stretch it to fit, patching any holes that might have formed.

Spread the herbed ricotta over the dough, leaving room for a crust to form on the edges, then top with the spinach, sliced mozzarella, tomatoes and a drizzle of olive oil across the crust and the pizza toppings. Sprinkle lightly with salt.

Bake for 20 to 25 minutes, or until the crust is cooked through and golden brown, then slice and serve. Top with red pepper flakes if you like a spicy bite.

SPINACH, BROCCOLI AND SCALLION PANCAKES WITH POACHED EGGS

These pancakes are not your traditional fried vegetable fritter. They are light, laced with delicious pieces of spinach, broccoli and scallions, and are perfect with a runny poached egg. If there are leftovers, they can be chopped and added to a sandwich or a salad for a delicious vegetable and protein boost.

SERVES 4

PANCAKES
1 ½ cups (137 g) chopped broccoli

4 cups (120 g) packed baby spinach

3 tbsp (45 ml) olive oil, divided

3 eggs

½ tsp baking soda

¼ cup (30 g) all-purpose flour

½ cup (54 g) panko breadcrumbs

½ cup (50 g) shredded Parmesan cheese

4 scallions, thinly sliced, divided

POACHED EGGS
4 cups (960 ml) water

4 large eggs

1 tbsp (15 ml) white vinegar

Preheat the oven to 375°F (190°C). Place a rimmed baking sheet in the oven to heat.

To make the pancakes: Steam the broccoli until tender but still crisp, about 3 to 5 minutes. While the broccoli cooks, sauté the spinach in 1 tablespoon (15 ml) of the olive oil in a skillet until wilted, about 3 minutes, then remove from the heat and roughly chop.

In a large bowl, scramble the eggs, and then add the baking soda, flour, panko and Parmesan cheese and stir to combine. Add the broccoli and spinach and half of the scallions. Mix to combine.

Remove the hot baking sheet from the oven and grease with the remaining 2 tablespoons (30 ml) olive oil. With an ice cream scoop, place pancakes evenly on the baking sheet. Gently press the top of each pancake to flatten. Bake for 10 minutes, then flip and bake for another 2 minutes, or until the centers of the pancakes are cooked through.

With about 8 minutes remaining on the pancakes, make the poached eggs: Boil the water in a large high-rimmed skillet. Once the water comes to a boil, crack each egg into its own ramekin. Add the white vinegar to the boiling water, reduce the heat to medium-low and drop each egg into the hot water. Cover the skillet and let the eggs cook for 3 minutes.

Remove the pancakes from the oven and serve 2 or 3 to a plate depending on their size. Top each plate with a poached egg and a sprinkle of the remaining scallions. Serve immediately.

TIP: If poaching all four eggs at once feels too daunting, try two at a time. Eggs cook quickly and this won't greatly delay your meal.

SPINACH PORTOBELLO MUSHROOMS WITH PARMESAN AND PANKO

Traditionally, stuffed mushrooms include a sausage and breadcrumb mixture. My version is much greener, much lighter and just as tasty! Using panko is a great way to introduce a buttery crunch. These vegetarian stuffed mushrooms make an excellent side dish or would be delicious atop whole-grain pasta.

SERVES 4

---

4 portobello mushroom caps, rubbed clean, stems trimmed evenly with gills

2 tbsp (30 ml) olive oil, divided

½ onion, diced

2 cloves garlic, minced

5 oz (144 g) baby spinach

¼ cup (14 g) thinly sliced sun-dried tomatoes

¼ cup (34 g) pitted and chopped olives (optional)

Salt to taste

1 tbsp (14 g) butter

¼ cup (27 g) panko breadcrumbs

¼ cup (25 g) shredded Parmesan or mozzarella cheese

Preheat the oven to 350°F (180°C).

Drizzle the mushrooms evenly with 1 tablespoon (15 ml) of the olive oil, place on a baking sheet gill side up and roast for 12 minutes, or until soft.

In a skillet, heat the remaining 1 tablespoon (15 ml) olive oil and sauté the onion until translucent, about 3 minutes. Add the garlic, spinach, tomatoes and olives (if using), and cook until the spinach is wilted, about 2 minutes; season to taste with salt.

Remove the mushroom caps from the oven, top with the spinach mixture, and roast for 3 minutes longer.

While the mushrooms are roasting, melt the butter over low heat, add the panko and toast until golden brown, about 2 minutes.

Combine the panko with the Parmesan cheese, top the mushrooms with the panko mixture and roast for 6 minutes longer.

Turn the broiler on high, and broil for 2 minutes to completely melt the cheese and further brown the panko. Watch this step very carefully as your broiler might be stronger or weaker than the average, and you don't want your toppings to burn.

Serve immediately.

TIPS: When shopping for mushrooms, look for caps that have defined sides—this will help your filling stay in place.

If your panko has smaller crumbs, run the breadcrumbs through a sifter so that you are left with larger pieces—these will crisp better.

If you're using olives, you might not need to season your spinach mixture with salt.

PENNE PASTA WITH PEAS AND LEMON PISTACHIO PESTO

I cannot get enough of this light and bright pesto! It's perfect on sandwiches, mixed into eggs and, of course, slathered on pasta. Is there anything better than pesto and pasta? I particularly love using different bases and nuts to enhance pesto flavors beyond the traditional basil and pine nut combination. This pesto recipes calls for quite a bit of lemon juice, but it really brings a fresh lightness and tanginess to this dish. Serving this dish with different textures creates an interesting finished product that's delicious hot or cold!

SERVES 4

PASTA

1 tbsp (15 ml) olive oil

1 lb (454 g) penne pasta

¾ cup (174 g) peas

¼ cup (25 g) thinly sliced scallion

2 tbsp (18 g) shelled pistachios

2 tbsp (13 g) shredded Parmesan cheese

PESTO

3 cups (90 g) baby spinach

6 tbsp (90 ml) olive oil

¼ cup (37 g) shelled pistachios

¼ cup (25 g) shredded Parmesan cheese

¼ cup (60 ml) lemon juice

2 cloves garlic

Salt to taste

To make the pasta: Bring a large pot of salted water to a boil, then add the olive oil and pasta. Cook the penne until it's al dente, 12 to 15 minutes.

While the pasta is cooking, make the pesto: Blend all the ingredients in a blender or food processor until smooth. Season to taste with salt and set aside.

When the pasta has about 2 minutes remaining, add the peas directly to the pasta water and let them cook.

Once the pasta is finished cooking, drain, reserving about ¼ cup (60 ml) of cooking liquid.

In a large bowl, combine the pasta and peas with the pesto, then toss to combine. If the sauce is too thick, add some of the cooking liquid and stir well to thin out the sauce.

Serve immediately, either family style or in individual bowls, topped with the scallions, pistachios and Parmesan cheese.

TIP: Frozen peas are perfect in this dish (and many others!).

RUSTIC EGG SANDWICH WITH SMOKED GOUDA, ROASTED GARLIC AND SAUTÉED SPINACH

Who doesn't love a good egg sandwich? Breakfast might be my favorite meal of the day, and I often order egg sandwiches in restaurants when we're out for breakfast or brunch. But, they are so easy to make at home—and this favorite is a staple in our house. If you have the patience, let the bread crisp really well so that you get a great crunch with each bite.

SERVES 4

---

1 head garlic, top quarter sliced off and discarded

1 tsp olive oil

8 tbsp (112 g) butter, divided

6 cups (180 g) baby spinach

8 slices whole-grain bread (a thick, hearty bread works best here)

1 cup (113 g) grated smoked Gouda cheese

4 large eggs

½ tsp salt

Preheat the oven to 375°F (190°C).

Place the garlic on a piece of aluminum foil and drizzle with the olive oil. Wrap into a pouch and roast for 30 to 40 minutes, or until the garlic is very soft and golden brown.

With about 15 minutes remaining on the garlic, heat 2 tablespoon (28 g) of the butter in a large skillet over medium heat and sauté the spinach until wilted, about 3 minutes; set aside.

Butter one side of 4 slices of bread with ½ tablespoon (7 g) of butter on each, top the other side with grated Gouda and place in the oven to melt, about 5 minutes.

While the cheese melts, heat 2 tablespoon (28 g) of butter in a large skillet and fry the eggs so that the whites are cooked but the yolks are still runny, about 3 minutes. If you prefer a cooked-through yolk, cook the egg a bit longer or flip halfway through to speed the yolk cooking. Season with salt.

Once the garlic is finished cooking, pop each clove out of the paper lining and mash into a paste, then spread evenly over the remaining 4 slices of bread. Flip and spread ½ tablespoon (7 g) of butter on each of those bread slices.

Heat a large skillet over medium heat (you can use the same one you used for the eggs) and begin to assemble the sandwiches by topping the garlic mash with sautéed spinach, a fried egg and the melted cheese toast. Place the sandwiches in the skillet to crisp the bread, gently flipping halfway through, about 3 minutes per side.

TIPS: Keeping roasted garlic on hand seriously cuts down on cooking time for this dish. Or, if you know you'd like to make this dish ahead of time, roast the garlic the day before and wrap in aluminum foil; it will last in the fridge for a couple of days.

If the egg yolks crack while you're flipping the sandwiches, do not fret! All the more rustic.

GEMELLI WITH LEMON BURRATA AND ESCAROLE

Burrata, a rich and oh so creamy mozzarella, is one of the many delicious Italian delicacies of which I just cannot get enough. Incredible alone, it's even more delicious when paired with other complementary flavors. Escarole is just hearty enough to stand up on its own, but plays so well with the creamy cheese and lemon flavor of the dish. Gemelli grips the melted cheese nicely, but your favorite shaped pasta would work well here, too.

SERVES 4

PASTA
1 tbsp (15 ml) olive oil

1 lb (454 g) gemelli pasta

SAUCE
2 tbsp (30 ml) olive oil

1 bunch escarole, roughly chopped

2 cloves garlic, minced

Zest of 2 lemons, divided

Juice of 2 lemons

8 oz (225 g) burrata or mozzarella cheese, diced

½ tsp salt (optional)

To make the pasta: Bring a large pot of salted water to a boil. Add the olive oil to the water, then add the pasta. Cook for 12 to 14 minutes for al dente pasta.

To make the sauce: In a large saucepan, heat the olive oil over medium-low heat. Sauté the escarole until it's just wilted, about 3 minutes, then add the garlic, stir and cook for 4 minutes.

Drain the pasta and add it to the garlic and escarole in the saucepan and stir to combine. Add the lemon juice and half the zest, then the burrata, and toss gently.

Season to taste with extra salt if needed, then serve immediately with the remaining lemon zest sprinkled on top.

ARUGULA BREAD SALAD

I can't stop eating this salad. The word obsession doesn't do it justice. It's a perfect summer treat—so refreshing, crunchy and delicious. The arugula is a perfect base for the big, savory flavors in this salad. Bring it to your friend's BBQ potluck or serve for a simple dinner with a grilled protein. I'd eat this every day if I could! Bonus points: It repurposes stale bread.

SERVES 4

VINAIGRETTE

1 tbsp (15 ml) honey mustard or whole-grain mustard

3 tbsp (45 ml) balsamic vinegar

¼ cup (60 ml) olive oil

¼ tsp salt, or more to taste

SALAD

3 cups (105 g) cubed stale or 2-day-old bread

2 tbsp (30 ml) olive oil

1 medium red onion, thinly sliced

2 medium tomatoes, sliced and seeded

1 medium cucumber, sliced and seeded

½ cup (84 g) chopped artichoke hearts

½ cup (68 g) chopped roasted red peppers

3 cups (60 g) arugula

½ cup (50 g) shredded Parmesan cheese

¼ cup (12 g) chopped chives

Preheat the oven to 350°F (180°C).

To make the vinaigrette: Combine the mustard and balsamic vinegar in a small bowl, then whisk in the olive oil and salt. Stir vigorously to mix.

To make the salad: Toss the cubed bread with the olive oil, spread on a baking sheet and bake for 10 to 15 minutes, or until golden brown and crispy.

While the bread bakes, assemble the vegetables, except for the arugula, in a large bowl.

Once the bread is baked, add it to the vegetables and toss with half the dressing. Add the arugula and the rest of the dressing, then toss well to combine.

Top with the Parmesan cheese and chives and serve immediately.

TIPS: This salad will keep in the fridge, but I think the taste and texture are best when served fresh. The vegetables and bread will begin to wilt and soften with time.

If you're looking for even more richness, sliced avocado would be delicious.

If you don't have stale bread at home, most bakeries or grocery stores will sell it at a discount.

OVEN-CRISPED POTATOES WITH SPINACH CHIMICHURRI

Because potatoes are often so bland, I decided to pair them with a very tangy chimichurri. You could add pickled jalapeños or red pepper flakes if you prefer a spicier kick, but the sauce is incredibly delicious as is. In our house, we like to serve these with brunch or dinner. They are versatile and do not require too much preparation time. They're perfect with poached eggs or in place of traditional mashed potatoes with simply roasted or grilled fish. Oh this dish! So yum.

SERVES 4

POTATOES
1 lb (254 g) small potatoes, scrubbed and pricked with a fork

2 tbsp (30 ml) olive oil, plus more for coating skillet

SPINACH CHIMICHURRI
¼ cup (60 ml) red wine vinegar

3 cloves garlic, diced

1 cup (16 g) chopped cilantro leaves (no stems)

½ cup (3 g) chopped parsley

½ cup (15 g) chopped raw spinach

¼ cup (60 ml) olive oil

Salt to taste

Preheat the oven to 450°F (230°C).

To make the potatoes: Place the potatoes in a large pot of water and bring to a boil; cook for 20 to 25 minutes, or until the potatoes are tender but not falling apart.

While the potatoes are cooking, make the chimichurri: Combine the vinegar, garlic, herbs and spinach in a blender or food processor, and process until smooth. Place in a bowl and whisk in the olive oil, season to taste with salt, set aside.

When the potatoes are finished cooking, drain them. Then with the bottom of a skillet or plate, gently press on the potatoes so that they break open, but still retain some of their shape—you are not mashing them; you are smashing them so they explode, but keep their general form. Brush potatoes with 2 tablespoons (30 ml) olive oil.

Grease a cast-iron skillet or cookie sheet with olive oil, transfer the smashed potatoes to the skillet or pan and bake for 8 minutes on each side, or until golden brown and crispy on the edges.

Top the hot, crispy potatoes with the spinach chimichurri and serve immediately with extra sauce on the side.

TIPS: I like using a cast-iron skillet because I think it conducts heat especially well, but if you don't have one at home, just use a simple cookie sheet.

Don't worry if the potatoes fall apart when you smash them; some may remain intact and others will not, but it will all taste the same.

Usually I don't mind using the cilantro stems in recipes because they have a lot of flavor, but here I found the stems to get stringy in the sauce.

WILTED ESCAROLE WITH DATES AND PECANS

Growing up, my mom would always make spinach with raisins and pine nuts. I craved it—literally—all the time, and she indulged me by making it often. It was so delicious: sweet, crunchy and just the right amount of savory. This recipe is a version of an elevated, childhood favorite.

SERVES 4

2 tbsp (30 ml) olive oil

1 head escarole, roughly chopped

¼ cup (34 g) whole pecans

¼ cup (37 g) sliced dates

¼ tsp salt

Heat the olive oil in a skillet over medium-low heat. Once the oil is hot, add the escarole and cook, covered, until the greens are wilted, 4 to 5 minutes.

With about 2 minutes remaining on the escarole, toast the pecans in a dry skillet over low heat until they are warmed and fragrant, about 2 minutes.

Toss the wilted escarole with the sliced dates, toasted pecans and salt. Serve warm.

TIP: I like each section of the escarole—the light and dark portions and the core. But if you prefer the outer layers, feel free to only use that part.

LEMON ARUGULA ORZO WITH CUCUMBERS AND FETA

Orzo makes for a very quick and easy meal. Since it cooks so fast, this dish is ready in no time. I love the crunch of the cucumbers, the saltiness of the feta and the slightly bitter bite of the arugula paired with the pillowy orzo pasta. This dish can be served at any temperature you like, making it versatile and really easy.

SERVES 4

PASTA

2 cups (480 ml) water

¾ cup (139 g) orzo pasta

1 medium cucumber, diced

½ cup (75 g) crumbled feta cheese

3 cups (60 g) arugula

Zest of ½ lemon

VINAIGRETTE

3 tbsp (45 ml) olive oil

Juice of 1 lemon

Salt to taste

To make the pasta: Bring the water to a boil in a pot, then add the orzo and cook for 10 minutes.

While the orzo is cooking, make the vinaigrette: Whisk all the ingredients together in a small bowl.

Strain the orzo, then rinse under cold water to chill; set aside.

In a large bowl, combine the vinaigrette, cucumber, feta and orzo. Add the arugula and toss. Season to taste with salt.

Serve the salad chilled or at room temperature, sprinkled with the lemon zest.

TIP: Make this dish your own: Add tomatoes, olives, capers, onions or artichoke hearts for even more flavor.

ASIAN PEANUT SLAW WITH AVOCADO

Cabbage might not be your go-to salad base, but it's really satisfying and incredibly affordable. I often make this slaw into a meal by adding cubed tofu or tempeh to round out the dish. If you're not keen on tofu or tempeh, grilled chicken would be an easy addition. I love the bite of the cabbage with crunchy peanuts and smooth avocado. If you like slaws on the spicy side, add your favorite tangy hot sauce!

SERVES 4

DRESSING

3 tbsp (45 ml) toasted sesame oil

1 tbsp (15 ml) soy sauce

1 tbsp (15 ml) lemon juice

1 tsp mild miso paste

1 tsp grated ginger

1 tsp grated garlic

SLAW

3 cups (210 g) shredded cabbage

1 cup (110 g) shredded carrot

½ cup (78 g) steamed edamame

¼ cup (37 g) shelled peanuts

¼ cup (25 g) thinly sliced scallion, divided

1 avocado, peeled, pitted and diced, divided

To make the dressing: Combine all the ingredients in a small bowl and whisk until blended. Set aside.

To make the slaw: In a large bowl, combine the cabbage, carrots and edamame.

Heat a skillet over medium-low heat and toast the peanuts until they are golden brown and warm, about 3 minutes.

Add half the peanuts and half the scallions to the slaw, then toss with the dressing. Gently fold in half the avocado.

Plate by topping with the remaining peanuts, scallions and avocado and serve immediately.

TIP: You can use shredded coleslaw mix if you are short on time.

DARK LEAFY GREENS

Dark leafy greens are some of the healthiest foods available—low in calories but rich in vitamins, minerals and fiber. Kale, collard greens, mustard greens, Swiss chard . . . the list goes on and on! Kale is one of my favorite greens to eat both raw and cooked, and you'll find both types of recipes in this chapter. It can be warm, comforting and satisfying, like the Rustic Kale Pesto Soup with Zucchini and White Beans (page 59), or light, crisp and refreshing, like the Farmers' Market Kale Salad with Apples and Radish (page 56).

It just goes to show how diverse dark leafy greens really can be. You don't just have to enjoy them as a mound of steamed greens; they can be a faux burrito wrapper, as in the Moo Shu Vegetables in Collard Green Wraps (page 64), or a luxurious brunch or light dinner, as in the Lacinato Kale and Caramelized Onion Galette (page 62).

Picking a favorite recipe is like picking a favorite child. But if you twist my arm, the Kale Salad with Candied Almonds, Apples and Maple Dressing (page 52) is a true favorite. I've made it over and over (and over!), and each time it's just as good as the last. Tangy, sweet, crisp and healthy—a match made in kitchen heaven!

WILTED GREENS AND SAUTÉED MUSHROOM CROSTINI

This is an ideal recipe to serve to cocktail party guests—it's simple, delicious and very easy. I prefer to use rainbow chard because the colors are so vibrant, but you could use any hearty green that you have available. Butter and olive oil create a perfect base to cook the mushrooms and the garlic, while wine and parsley bathe the mushrooms in such incredible flavor. I could eat this dish for days!

SERVES 4

3 tbsp (42 g) butter, divided

2 tbsp (30 ml) olive oil, plus more for drizzling

8 oz (225 g) sliced cremini mushrooms

2 cloves garlic, minced

¼ cup (60 ml) white wine (I like to use Sauvignon Blanc)

4 tbsp (16 g) fresh parsley, divided

1 cup (30 g) chopped rainbow chard, thick center stems discarded

1 baguette, sliced

Melt 2 tablespoons (28 g) of the butter and the olive oil in a large pan, then add the sliced mushrooms and garlic, and cook for about 3 minutes, or until softened.

Add the white wine and 3 tablespoons (12 g) of the parsley to the mushrooms and stir to combine. Continue cooking the mushrooms until most of the liquid has evaporated, about 10 minutes. With 4 minutes left, add the rainbow chard and the remaining 1 tablespoon (14 g) butter.

Turn the broiler on high, spread the bread slices on a baking sheet and toast until golden brown, 3 to 5 minutes, depending on the strength of your broiler, then drizzle with olive oil.

Top each slice of bread with the mushroom mixture and garnish with a sprinkle of the remaining 1 tablespoon (4 g) parsley, then serve immediately.

TIPS: If you're feeling adventurous, using a wild mushroom mix would be delicious and gorgeous to serve.

When cooking, always use a wine you will drink! The flavor intensifies, so if it's not good enough to drink, it's not good enough to cook with.

If you want a bit more garlicky bite, rub the crostini with a raw garlic clove when it comes out of the oven, before you spoon on the topping.

MUSTARD GREEN AND WHITE BEAN HUMMUS WITH SPICED PITA CHIPS

White beans are deliciously creamy, abundantly available and so inexpensive. I frequently stock up on canned beans when I see them on sale at the market. They have a long shelf life, are a perfect addition to soups, stews and salads and are of course a great base for dips! They can be salty, so be sure to rinse them well, but they are a delicious, versatile source of protein and fiber. Instead of using chickpeas like a traditional hummus, my white bean hummus is creamier and lighter, and it's green—thanks to the mustard greens! Served with warm homemade pita chips, this dish is a cocktail party (or after-school snack, pre-dinner munch . . .) knockout—boom!

SERVES 4

HUMMUS

1 can (15 oz [420 g]) white beans, rinsed and drained

2 cups (134 g) torn mustard green leaves, center stems discarded

2 cloves garlic

⅓ cup (80 ml) olive oil

¼ cup (60 ml) lemon juice

½ tsp salt, or more to taste

PITA CHIPS

2 tbsp (30 ml) olive oil, plus more for drizzling

¼ tsp salt

¼ tsp ground cumin

¼ tsp smoked paprika

2 large whole-wheat pitas with pockets, quartered and sliced in half to make 8 triangles each

Preheat the oven to 350°F (180°C).

To make the hummus: Combine all the ingredients in a blender or food processor and process until well incorporated. If you prefer a bit of texture in your hummus, combine until you have a creamy texture but can still see visible bits of white beans and mustard greens. Season with salt to taste and set aside.

To make the pita chips: In a small bowl, whisk together the oil and spices, then gently brush the pita triangles with the seasoned oil. Drizzle with extra oil, spread on a baking sheet and bake for 10 to 12 minutes, or until the chips are golden brown and crispy.

Serve the hummus with the warm pita chips fresh from the oven.

TIPS: If you have an olive oil spray bottle in your kitchen, giving each chip an extra misting of oil (instead of the pre-baking drizzle) is ideal. If not, very lightly drizzle a few extra drops on each chip.

If mustard greens are too strong for your taste, substitute kale for a milder flavor.

KALE SALAD WITH CANDIED ALMONDS, APPLES AND MAPLE DRESSING

I'm all about sweet and salty flavors together. So when I came up with this recipe, it was my heaven in a bowl. I love the crunchy apples and almonds, the soft and tangy feta and the hearty bite of kale. The lemon juice cuts the sweetness of both the nuts and the maple syrup, but bounces nicely off the tart apple. Oh, I could go on and on. But, I'll let you get started so you can go on and on!

SERVES 4

DRESSING

¼ cup (60 ml) olive oil

2 tbsp (30 ml) maple syrup

¼ cup (60 ml) lemon juice

Salt to taste

CANDIED ALMONDS

½ cup (69 g) whole raw almonds

1 tbsp (15 ml) olive oil

1 tbsp (15 ml) maple syrup

½ tsp salt

SALAD

1 bunch kale, stems discarded and leaves roughly chopped

½ cup (75 g) crumbled feta cheese

4 scallions, thinly sliced

1 medium tart apple (Granny Smith, Northern Spy or Braeburn), halved, cored and thinly sliced

Preheat the oven to 300°F (148°C).

To make the dressing: Combine all the ingredients in a bowl and whisk until well incorporated, then set aside.

To make the candied almonds: In a bowl, toss the almonds with the olive oil, maple syrup and salt, spread in one flat layer on a parchment- or foil-lined cookie sheet and bake for 10 minutes.

To make the salad: In a large bowl, combine the kale, feta, scallions, apple and warm almonds, toss with the dressing and serve immediately.

TIP: If you don't have almonds, you can use any other nuts you have on hand—pecans or walnuts would be delicious.

KALE CAESAR WITH CHALLAH CROUTONS

Kale may be the vegetable fad du jour these days, but it was a favorite of mine long before it became fashionable. Flavorful, versatile, low in calories and rich in vitamins A, K and C, kale is a nutrient powerhouse. This dish is gorgeous when made with red kale, but plain green curly kale works just as well. Paired with this homemade dressing, it brings the tastes of a traditional Caesar salad without all the calories and fat. Because kale is a hearty green, it holds up especially nicely against the thick and flavorful dressing. Now that kale appears prominently on almost every restaurant menu, it's time to demystify this go-to green and make a delicious kale salad at home. Wow your guests with homemade dressing and croutons. They are simple (but your guests don't have to know that!).

SERVES 4

DRESSING

¾ cup (103 g) raw cashews, soaked in water to cover and refrigerated for at least 12 hours

5 tbsp (75 ml) water

2 tbsp (30 ml) lemon juice

2 tbsp (17 g) capers, drained of brine

1 tsp Dijon mustard

2 cloves garlic

2 tbsp (12 g) grated Parmesan cheese

2 tbsp (34 g) mild miso paste

¼ tsp salt, or more to taste

CROUTONS

2 cups (70 g) cubed challah bread

1 tbsp (15 ml) olive oil

⅛ tsp salt

GREENS

1 large bunch kale, stems discarded and leaves ripped into bite-size pieces

Lemon wedges, for serving

Preheat the oven to 375°F (190°C).

To make the dressing: In a blender, combine all the dressing ingredients and blend until very smooth, scraping the sides of the blender for even texture. If the consistency of the dressing is too thick for your liking, mix in additional water, 1 tablespoon (15 ml) at a time, until you are satisfied, then set aside.

To make the croutons: Toss the bread cubes with the olive oil and season with salt. Spread on a baking sheet and bake the croutons for 12 minutes, or until golden brown and crunchy.

To make the greens: In a large bowl, combine the kale with half the dressing; if you prefer a lighter or heavier dressed salad, adjust the volume of dressing to your taste. With very clean hands, massage the dressing into the kale until it is well combined.

Top the salad with the challah croutons and a lemon wedge. Serve individually or family style, adding any leftover dressing for extra flavor.

TIPS: For a vegan-friendly recipe, omit the Parmesan cheese and swap vegan bread for the challah. You may wish to increase the amount of salt a bit, to compensate for the lack of cheese.

The dressing can be made ahead of time and stored in the refrigerator for up to a week.

FARMERS' MARKET KALE SALAD WITH APPLES AND RADISH

I'm a farmers' market junkie—in the best possible way! I cannot ever resist the colorful produce, fresh flowers or artisan cheese and breads: a foodie's heaven. This salad is sweet and savory, crunchy and smooth, flavorful yet light. If you haven't ever experimented with radishes before, they are delicious—crispy and crunchy and just the tiniest bit bitter. I love pairing raw radishes with something sweet, and the apples in this salad balance perfectly.

SERVES 4

DRESSING
¼ cup (60 g) tahini paste

¼ cup (60 ml) lemon juice

Salt to taste

SALAD
10 oz (284 g) kale, chopped

4 medium radishes, halved and thinly sliced

2 sweet apples, such as Honeycrisp, cored and diced

½ cup (75 g) crumbled feta cheese

½ cup (90 g) white beans, rinsed

2 tbsp (6 g) chopped chives

To make the dressing: In a large bowl, whisk the tahini paste and lemon juice together, then add salt to taste.

To make the salad: Add the kale to the dressing and mix well with your hands or two spoons.

Add the radishes, apples, feta, beans and chives and toss well. Serve immediately.

TIP: If you're looking for an extra crunch, try adding your favorite nut.

RUSTIC KALE PESTO SOUP WITH ZUCCHINI AND WHITE BEANS

Soup is a quick lunch or dinner, perfect for guests and easy enough for weeknight cooking. This soup is rich and creamy while remaining light, thanks to puréed white beans taking the place of cream or milk. The pesto flavor is perfectly fresh and bright against the earthy tones of the beans and kale. And I know it goes without saying, but soup really does get better with time—this is a delicious make-ahead meal. I especially like this soup served alongside griddled, crusty bread, perfect for dipping.

SERVES 4

SOUP

1 medium white onion, diced

2 cloves garlic, minced

2 tbsp (30 ml) olive oil, divided

4 cups (280 g) kale, stems discarded and leaves roughly chopped

1 large zucchini, quartered and diced

3 cups (710 ml) low-sodium vegetable stock or broth

1 can (15 oz [420 g]) white beans, drained and rinsed, divided

1 cup (145 g) frozen peas

Salt to taste

Lemon juice, for drizzling

Parmesan cheese, for garnish

Red pepper flakes (optional)

PESTO

1 bunch basil

½ cup (50 g) grated Parmesan cheese

½ cup (70 g) cashews, toasted

1 clove garlic, roughly chopped

¼ cup (60 ml) olive oil

2 tbsp (30 ml) lemon juice

To make the soup: In a large heavy-bottomed pot, sauté the onion and garlic in 1 tablespoon (15 ml) of the olive oil over low heat until soft and translucent, 5 to 7 minutes.

Add the kale and zucchini to the onion mixture and sauté with the remaining 1 tablespoon (15 ml) olive oil, stirring frequently, for about 3 minutes. Add the stock and 1 cup (240 g) of the white beans to the pot and continue to let it simmer.

Meanwhile, make the pesto: Combine all the pesto ingredients in a blender or food processor and process until smooth and creamy; set aside.

Place the remaining ¾ cup (180 g) beans in your blender or food processor (no need to wash it after making the pesto) and blend until smooth. Add the puréed beans to the soup to thicken it, and stir well.

Add half the pesto to the pot and bring the soup to a boil, then turn down the heat to medium, cover and cook until the vegetables are soft and the stock has reduced by a third, about 10 minutes. Add the peas and cook for another 5 minutes, then season to taste with salt. Remove the soup from the heat and let cool for a few minutes.

With a ladle, add the soup to the blender or food processor in batches and pulse three or four times to break up the vegetables; do not overblend, as this soup should be served chunky.

Serve with a dollop of pesto, lemon juice squeezed over the top, a sprinkle of Parmesan cheese and red pepper flakes if you like an extra kick.

RAINBOW CHARD AND PARMESAN QUICHE

Rainbow chard is not only gorgeous but also delicious! Paired with garlic, eggs and cheese in this quiche, it imparts a subtle, earthy flavor. While the crust is beyond buttery, flaky and flavorful, the custard filling is very light and airy. Perfect when served with a simple salad, this quiche makes an excellent light meal.

My nana was an amazing cook and baker. She had a big family to feed and mastered simple yet delicious cooking. Her most famous recipe was for apple pie; the crust and filling were so good. Each time I make a pastry dough I think of her, and this quiche recipe is no different. The china pictured here is also hers—there's lots of my grandmother in this recipe!

SERVES 4 TO 8

CRUST

1 ¼ cups (156 g) all-purpose flour

¾ tsp salt

½ cup (112 g) cold butter, cubed

5 tbsp (75 ml) cold water, or more as needed

FILLING

2 ½ cups (175 g) chopped rainbow chard leaves, very bottom stems discarded

2 tbsp (30 ml) olive oil

2 cloves garlic, minced

½ white onion, diced

¼ tsp salt

4 large eggs

½ cup (120 ml) whole milk

¾ cup (75 g) shredded Parmesan cheese

EGG WASH

1 egg

1 tbsp (15 ml) water

To make the crust: Combine the flour and salt in a large bowl. Using a pastry cutter, work the butter into the flour until combined. Add the cold water, 1 tablespoon (15 ml) at a time, mixing well after each addition. The dough should not be sticky, but if you squeeze it, it should hold together and not crumble. If the dough won't come together, add more water, 1 tablespoon (15 ml) at a time.

Wrap the dough in plastic wrap and refrigerate for at least 30 minutes.

To make the filling: While the dough rests, in a skillet over medium heat, sauté the rainbow chard in the olive oil until the greens are just beginning to wilt, about 2 minutes. Add the garlic and onion and continue cooking until the greens are completely wilted, another 3 to 4 minutes, then add the salt, stir to combine and set aside.

Whisk the eggs and milk together until well combined. Add the cooked rainbow chard and Parmesan cheese, stir to combine and then set aside.

Preheat the oven to 375°F (190°C).

Once the dough has rested, roll it out on a floured workspace until it is at least 11 inches (28 cm) in diameter. Place the dough over an 8-inch (20-cm) pie plate and gently press it into the sides and bottom. Fold the extra dough over to form the rim of the crust. With your right index finger, thumb and left index finger's knuckle (or a fork), make gentle indents every inch (2.5 cm) on the crust.

Prick the bottom of the crust with a fork and bake for 12 minutes. Then remove the crust from the oven. Gently pour the filling into the parbaked pie crust. If the chard is uneven, use a spatula to evenly distribute it in the custard.

To make the egg wash: Whisk together the egg and water in a small bowl. Brush the egg wash on the rim of the pie crust.

Bake for 35 to 40 minutes, or until the center of the quiche is set and the crust is golden brown. Let it sit for about 5 minutes, then slice and serve warm.

LACINATO KALE AND CARAMELIZED ONION GALETTE

Savory pies are easy for a group and a crowd-pleaser, and this one is very savory, very pleasing and filled with healthy greens! Lacinato kale is especially hearty and the exposed parts of the kale crisp up beautifully under the heat of the oven. If you aren't a fan of salty feta, your favorite cheese should work, but I really love the extra savory bite of the feta.

SERVES 4

CRUST

1 ¼ cups (156 g) all-purpose flour

¾ tsp salt

½ cup (112 g) cold butter, cubed

5 tbsp (75 ml) cold water, or more as needed

FILLING

2 onions, thinly sliced

2 tbsp (28 g) butter

¼ tsp salt, divided

2 tbsp (30 ml) olive oil, divided

1 bunch lacinato kale, center stems discarded and leaves roughly chopped

½ cup (75 g) feta cheese, plus more for garnish

EGG WASH

1 egg

1 tbsp (15 ml) water

TIP: If you are short on time, you may place your crust in the freezer for about 20 minutes, but watch it! If left too long, the dough will freeze, which won't be a time-saver for tonight's dinner.

To make the crust: Combine the flour and salt in a large bowl. Using a pastry cutter, work the butter into the flour until combined. Add the cold water, 1 tablespoon (15 ml) at a time, mixing well after each addition. The dough should not be sticky, but if you squeeze it, it should hold together and not crumble. If the dough won't come together, add more water, 1 tablespoon (15 ml) at a time.

Wrap the dough in plastic wrap and refrigerate for at least 30 minutes.

To make the filling: While the dough rests, in a medium-size sauté pan over low heat, caramelize the onions with the butter and ⅛ teaspoon of salt. Cook for about 3 minutes, then add 1 tablespoon (15 ml) of the olive oil and continue to cook the onions until they are golden brown and very tender, at least 15 minutes. Scrape into a bowl and set aside.

Turn the heat to medium-low, and using the same skillet, sauté the kale in the remaining 1 tablespoon (15 ml) olive oil, season with the remaining ⅛ teaspoon salt. Cook until the greens are completely wilted, about 8 minutes. If your kale is browning too quickly, add 1 tablespoon (15 ml) water and cover the pan to allow the kale to steam.

Preheat the oven to 375°F (190°C).

Once the dough has chilled, roll it out on a floured workspace until it is about ¼ inch (6.5 mm) thick. Place the dough on a nonstick silicone or parchment paper–lined baking sheet. Scatter the feta cheese on the bottom of the crust leaving 1 inch (2.5 cm) of room from the edge of the crust to the filling to fold the crust over. Top the feta with the kale and caramelized onions, then fold the extra crust up over the kale as far as it will go.

To make the egg wash: Whisk together the egg and water in a small bowl, then brush onto the crust.

Bake for 40 to 45 minutes, or until the crust is golden brown and flaky. Top the tart with extra feta cheese and serve immediately.

BAKED EGGS WITH FETA AND KALE

I grew up eating baked eggs—my mom loved to make them and our family loved to eat them! I was anything but a picky eater, but when your child enjoys a nourishing, easy to prepare meal, it quickly becomes a go-to in your playbook. My mom made baked eggs in muffin tins—the simple aluminum kind, not the fancier nonstick versions we use today. Somehow the eggs always slipped out of each cavity so easily. It was like a magic trick for my young eyes! My take on baked eggs substitutes milk for cream, and adds a healthy dose of green hiding at the bottom. Also, I use ramekins in lieu of muffin tins, because I have a ramekin obsession. Admitting it is the first step.

SERVES 4

2 cups (140 g) kale, leaves torn, center stems discarded

3 tbsp (45 ml) olive oil, divided

¼ cup (38 g) feta cheese

½ cup (120 ml) whole milk

8 eggs

Salt to taste

Toast, to serve (optional)

Green salad, to serve (optional)

Preheat the oven to 350°F (180°C).

In a skillet over medium-low heat, sauté the kale in 1 tablespoon (15 ml) of the olive oil until wilted, about 5 minutes.

Grease 4 ramekins with the remaining 2 tablespoons (30 ml) olive oil. Place an even amount of kale in each ramekin and top with 1 tablespoon (9 g) of feta cheese and 2 tablespoons (30 ml) of milk. Crack 2 eggs into each ramekin, sprinkle with salt and then bake for 24 minutes, or until the whites are set. Serve immediately in the ramekins with toast or a green salad.

TIP: Be sure to use ramekins that are at least 3 ½ inches (9 cm) tall or larger—the tiny ones won't hold the filling.

MOO SHU VEGETABLES IN COLLARD GREEN WRAPS

Living in New York City, we have no shortage of amazing Asian restaurants. And when we opt for Chinese, which is a favorite in our family, moo shu vegetables are my go-to dish. It tends to be a lighter option than many others on the menu, and it's packed with vegetables—two things I really love. My version swaps the traditional crepe-style wrap for collard greens, which create a perfect vehicle to serve the sweet and sour vegetables. Just as good as takeout, healthier and faster, this recipe is an easy weeknight choice.

SERVES 4

SAUCE

¼ cup (60 ml) hoisin sauce

1 tbsp (15 ml) toasted sesame oil

1 tbsp (15 ml) soy sauce

1 tbsp (15 ml) seasoned rice vinegar

MOO SHU VEGETABLES

2 eggs, beaten

1 tsp plus 2 tbsp (35 ml) sesame oil, divided

4 cloves garlic, minced

2 tsp (10 g) finely grated ginger

3 cups (210 g) sliced mushrooms

1 cup (160 g) sliced onion

1 cup (120 g) shredded carrot

1 head savoy cabbage, cored and shredded

1 bunch scallions, thinly sliced on the bias, divided

8 large collard green leaves, thick lower stems removed (you will be left with a triangular-shaped opening at the bottom of each leaf)

To make the sauce: In a small bowl, whisk the ingredients together until well incorporated. Reserve 2 tablespoons (30 ml) and set aside.

To make the vegetables: In a large skillet over low heat, scramble the eggs in 1 teaspoon of the sesame oil, remove from the pan, roughly chop and set aside. Wipe out the skillet to reuse it for the vegetables.

Heat the remaining 2 tablespoons (30 ml) oil in the skillet, add the garlic and ginger, and cook until fragrant, about 2 minutes, then add the mushrooms, onion and carrot and cook for 4 minutes.

Add the cabbage and reserved 2 tablespoons (30 ml) of sauce, adjust the heat to medium and cook, covered, until the cabbage is wilted, about 5 minutes.

Add the cooked eggs and half the scallions to the cabbage mixture, and stir to combine.

Spread the remaining sauce evenly on each collard green, spoon the vegetables onto the wrap and roll as tightly as possible to enclose.

Slice in half with a serrated knife, garnish with the remaining scallions and serve immediately.

CRISPY TOFU COLLARD GREEN TACOS WITH PEANUT SAUCE

I started making a version of this dish years ago with rice paper wrappers instead of collard green leaves. But I was inspired by a trip to Koreatown (where the barbecue is served in lettuce cups rather than a grain-based vessel), and I've really come to love the freshness and crunch of the green vegetable instead of the softness of the summer roll wrapper. Since collard greens are hearty, they hold the contents of these tacos perfectly. By using panko breadcrumbs and baking the tofu, there's an amazing faux-fried crispness.

SERVES 4

PEANUT DIPPING SAUCE

½ cup (84 g) peanut butter

1 tbsp plus 1 tsp (20 ml) soy sauce

1 tbsp plus 1 tsp (20 ml) lime juice

1 tbsp plus 1 tsp (20 ml) hoisin sauce

¼ cup (60 ml) water

Salt to taste

TACOS

1 block (16 oz [455 g]) extra-firm tofu

1 large egg

2 tsp (10 ml) water

1 cup (108 g) panko crumbs

2 tbsp (16 g) black sesame seeds

1 large sweet potato, roasted or cooked in the microwave until soft

1 avocado, peeled and pitted

8 large collard green leaves, thick lower stems removed (you will be left with a triangular-shaped opening at the bottom of each leaf)

1 bunch scallions, thinly sliced on the bias

1 medium cucumber, peeled and thinly sliced into matchsticks

Preheat the oven to 400°F (200°C).

To make the peanut dipping sauce: Combine the ingredients in a blender or food processor and process until well incorporated. Season to taste with salt and set aside.

To make the tacos: Remove the tofu block from its package and slice into 8 pieces. Slice each piece in half widthwise to make 16 rectangles, then pat dry with a paper towel.

Beat together the egg and the water and add it to a wide, shallow dish, then mix the panko and sesame seeds and add them to a second shallow dish.

Coat each tofu slice in the egg, then dip in the panko-sesame mixture, coating evenly on each side (including the edges).

Coat an aluminum foil–lined cookie sheet with cooking spray, then bake the tofu sticks for about 20 minutes, turning them over as necessary, until golden brown and crisp.

While the tofu bakes, halve and peel the sweet potato and slice it into sticks.

Mash the avocado and spread evenly over each collard green leaf. Sprinkle with the scallions, then evenly stack the cucumbers and sweet potatoes and top with the baked tofu. Wrap the leaf as tightly as you can, then slice in half and serve with the peanut dipping sauce.

*See photo on page 46.

SUN-DRIED TOMATO RICOTTA RIGATONI WITH KALE AND WHITE WINE

This meal is an excellent way to create a tasty, nutritious and cohesive dish from pantry items and other ingredients you always have available. For a New Yorker such as myself (space is at a premium!), there are few things more satisfying than creating a meal while avoiding a trip to the store and using up forgotten items taking up space in the pantry. Sun-dried tomatoes add a great depth of flavor to so many dishes, and are great to have on hand year-round. This dish is colorful and bursting with bold flavors from the sun-dried tomatoes, white wine and creamy ricotta.

SERVES 4

WHITE WINE SAUCE

1 head garlic, top quarter sliced off and discarded

2 tbsp (30 ml) olive oil, divided

1 onion, thinly sliced

3 cups (210 g) kale, leaves torn, center stems discarded

½ cup (120 ml) dry white wine

4 tbsp (56 g) butter

12 sun-dried tomatoes, thinly sliced

2 tbsp (16 g) all-purpose flour

¾ cup (180 ml) whole milk

¼ cup (62 g) ricotta cheese

Salt to taste

¼ cup (11 g) thinly sliced basil

PASTA

1 tbsp (15 ml) olive oil

1 lb (455 g) rigatoni

TIP: Sun-dried tomatoes come packed in oil, air-dried or vacuum-sealed. For this recipe, look for ones packed in oil or vacuum-sealed. I find the air-dried tomatoes a bit too chewy.

Preheat the oven to 375°F (190°C).

To make the sauce: Place the garlic on a piece of aluminum foil and drizzle with 1 teaspoon of the olive oil. Wrap into a pouch and roast for 30 to 40 minutes, or until the garlic is soft and golden brown.

In a saucepan, sauté the onion in the remaining 1 tablespoon and 2 teaspoons (25 ml) olive oil over medium-low heat until soft and beginning to turn golden, 6 to 8 minutes. Add the kale and mix to combine. Cook for 3 to 4 minutes longer, or until the kale has wilted. Remove from the pan and set aside.

Add the white wine to deglaze the pan and raise the heat so that the wine begins to bubble and releases any fond that has formed on the bottom of the pan (don't be afraid to scrape that deliciousness off with a wooden spoon). Add the butter and sun-dried tomatoes, then cook until the butter melts.

Add the flour to the wine and butter mixture and whisk well. The sauce will become very thick at this point. Add the milk a few splashes at a time, and continue to whisk until the milk is incorporated.

Once the garlic finishes roasting, remove from the oven and pop each clove out of its paper wrapping. Mash the garlic, then chop it and add it to the sauce along with the ricotta. Stir well, cover and reduce the heat to the lowest setting. Season to taste with salt.

To make the pasta: Bring a large pot of salted water to a boil. Add the olive oil and then add the pasta. Cook for 12 to 14 minutes for al dente. Once the pasta is finished, drain the cooking liquid but reserve at least ½ cup (120 ml).

Place the pasta back into the pot it was cooked in, add the kale, onions and white wine sauce, and stir to combine. If the sauce is too thick, add some of the reserved cooking liquid to thin it out. Serve immediately topped with fresh basil.

GREEN GODDESS KALE, TWO WAYS

Kale chips are one of my favorite ways to eat kale—they are crispy, crunchy, satisfying and dip-able! I love vegetables I can dip. This recipe highlights kale's versatility and different textures by combining baked kale chips and raw kale with a super-flavorful—tangy, garlicky and herby—green goddess–style dressing and creamy white beans.

SERVES 4

DRESSING

1 tsp plus ¼ cup (65 ml) olive oil, divided

1 head garlic, top quarter cut off and discarded

1 cup (245 g) low-fat Greek yogurt

½ cup (120 ml) lemon juice

½ cup (12 g) fresh basil

½ cup (50 g) chopped scallion

1 tsp salt

SALAD

1 bunch kale, leaves torn, center stems discarded, divided

1 tbsp (15 ml) olive oil

¾ cup (180 g) white beans, rinsed and drained

1 cup (149 g) sliced tomatoes

Preheat the oven to 375°F (190°C).

To make the dressing: Drizzle 1 teaspoon of the olive oil on the garlic, then wrap in aluminum foil and roast for 30 to 40 minutes.

Turn the oven down to 350°F (180°C).

Pop the garlic out of its paper wrapping and add to a blender or food processor along with all the remaining dressing ingredients; process until well incorporated. If you prefer a bit of texture in your salad dressing, combine until you have a creamy texture but can still see visible bits of basil. Set aside.

To make the salad: Massage 2 large handfuls of very dry kale with the olive oil. Place on a baking sheet and cook for about 12 minutes, or until they are crispy, chip-like and easily move when you shake the baking sheet.

In a large bowl, toss the remaining raw kale with half the dressing. With clean hands, rub the kale and dressing together until well combined and the kale glistens with an even coating of dressing. Add the beans and tomatoes, then top with the kale chips, leaving some whole and crunching others up with your fingers. Drizzle more dressing on top and serve immediately.

OTHER GREEN GOODIES

While I love all manner of "leafy greens," there are plenty of other green vegetables that deserve some love and attention, too. I could go on and on about the plethora of green goodies ranging from A to Z (quite literally, in fact!): asparagus to zucchini. The variety and versatility of these vegetables is stunning. They deserve to be elevated and enjoyed more than merely chopping them into a salad or steaming them blandly as a throw-away side dish. They are versatile enough to star as the hearty main course, as a refreshing soup or scene-stealing accompaniment, or even to augment your favorite dishes with vitamins, nutrients and fiber. They may even show up in some unexpected places. My Double Chocolate Zucchini Muffins (page 90) are so decadent. I bet if you blindfolded someone and asked what was folded into the muffin, you would get many guesses, none of which would be a member of the squash family! And for all you moms, you should never pass up an opportunity to fortify recipes for the family with additional goodness. Extra nutrition never tasted so good.

GREEN HEIRLOOM TOMATOES WITH MOZZARELLA AND NECTARINES

This is an updated version of a traditional Caprese salad—and sweeter! People often associate fruit with dessert and sweet applications, but sweet summer fruits pair fabulously with a savory cheese. Heirloom tomatoes are abundant in the summer, often vary in shape and are available in many gorgeous colors ranging from deep reds to bright yellows and striped green, as I've used here. Mix and match your ingredients to create your masterpiece against the white canvas of the mozzarella.

SERVES 4

1 cup (240 ml) balsamic vinegar

2 medium green heirloom tomatoes

2 medium nectarines

8 oz (226 g) fresh mozzarella cheese

Kosher or flaky salt to taste

In a small saucepan, bring the balsamic vinegar to a boil over high heat. As soon as it comes to a boil, adjust the heat to medium-low and cook until the balsamic vinegar is reduced and very thick (by about half of the original amount), 10 to 12 minutes. Set aside to cool.

While the balsamic vinegar cools, slice the tomatoes, nectarines and mozzarella cheese with a serrated knife.

Arrange the tomatoes, nectarines and cheese in an alternating pattern on a plate, then drizzle the reduced balsamic vinegar over the salad and sprinkle with the flaky salt. Serve immediately.

TIPS: I like to cut off the round ends of both the tomatoes and the nectarines as I find it's easier to layer the fruits when there is a uniform edge.

If the balsamic reduction cools too much and becomes hard, pop it into the microwave for 10 to 15 seconds to help it soften.

ASPARAGUS AND EGG PUFF PASTRY

This dish keeps everything contained in one place, which means really easy serving and cleanup! What more could you ask for as a busy home cook? This dish does double duty and can be an appetizer or an entree. On weekends, serve this pastry with a fresh salad and a breakfast cocktail and you've got yourself a delicious and elegant brunch that will wow your friends.

SERVES 4

1 sheet all-butter puff pastry

8 oz (226 g) fresh mozzarella cheese, shredded

1 bunch asparagus, woody stems discarded

2 tbsp (30 ml) olive oil

5 eggs, divided

Salt to taste

Red pepper flakes (optional)

Thaw the puff pastry for 30 to 40 minutes, or until the dough is cold but pliable. Unfold the dough and immediately place it on a greased nonstick baking sheet or parchment paper–lined baking sheet.

Preheat the oven to 375°F (190°C).

Top the raw dough with the shredded mozzarella, then the asparagus. Drizzle the olive oil over the top. Beat 1 of the eggs in a bowl and brush the crust with it, then bake until golden brown and puffed, about 30 minutes.

With 10 minutes left on the timer, remove the puff pastry from the oven, crack the remaining 4 eggs in each corner of the pastry and bake until the whites are set. Be gentle! The eggs can easily slide off the pastry. If the whites are not set after 10 minutes, leave the pastry in until they are set—it's fine to let the crust bake a bit longer.

Sprinkle with salt as soon as it comes out of the oven, then slice into squares or rectangles using a knife or pizza cutter. Serve with red pepper flakes on the side for diners to use if they wish.

TIP: Try sprinkling the puff pastry crust with cheese before baking for a crunchy and cheesy bite.

COOL CUCUMBER SALAD WITH DILL AND RED ONION

Anything that is pickled, tart and cold is bound to be a winner in our house. This cucumber salad is just the right balance of sweet and tart, and is deliciously refreshing on a hot summer day. Slightly more elevated that traditional pickles, this dish can really add delicious tang to almost any meal. It would be perfect atop my Veggie Burgers with Farro (page 114).

SERVES 4

DRESSING

1 tbsp (15 ml) olive oil

1 tbsp (15 ml) red wine vinegar

1 tsp granulated sugar

SALAD

6 mini seedless or 2 large regular cucumbers

1 small red onion

2 tbsp (1 g) chopped dill, divided

Salt to taste

To make the dressing: Combine all of the dressing ingredients in a bowl and whisk to dissolve the sugar.

To make the salad: Thinly slice the cucumbers using your sharpest knife. I find that a cleaver-shaped knife grips the cucumber best, allowing you to create thin, even slices. Don't worry if yours are not even—rustic works here, too. Toss the sliced cucumbers with the dressing and set aside.

Thinly slice the red onion, using your sharpest knife again. Add it to the cucumber mixture and top with three-fourths of the dill. Toss to combine. Taste the salad and add salt to taste—just be aware that the flavors will intensify as they sit, so be conservative.

Cover the salad and refrigerate for at least 1 hour. Serve sprinkled with the remaining chopped dill.

*See photo on page 70.

TIPS: Sharp knives are actually safer than dull knives. Still, be sure to watch what you are doing and take your time—it's not a race.

You can make this recipe ahead of time, but just know that the longer salted cucumber sits in the bowl, the more water it will release, which will water down the dressing. So if you make it ahead of time, season it before serving.

ROASTED ZUCCHINI SALAD WITH FETA AND WHITE BEANS

Zucchini is such a mild-tasting vegetable that I enjoy it best when it's paired with bold flavors. This salad hits all my favorite notes—creamy, tangy, tart, crispy and sweet! I especially like recipes that are easy to edit to your tastes: Swap the cheese or the beans or add in your favorite fresh herb. This salad won't disappoint!

SERVES 4

SALAD

2 large zucchini, diced

1 tbsp (15 ml) olive oil

1 small red onion, thinly sliced

1 pint (298 g) cherry tomatoes, halved

1 can (15 oz [420 g]) white beans, rinsed and drained

½ cup (75 g) crumbled feta cheese

DRESSING

2 tbsp (30 ml) olive oil

1 tbsp (15 ml) red wine vinegar

1 tbsp (15 ml) lemon juice

½ tsp oregano

½ tsp garlic powder

Salt to taste

Preheat the oven to 375°F (190°C).

To make the salad: Toss the zucchini with the olive oil, place in an even layer on a baking sheet and roast until golden brown and cooked through, about 30 minutes. To finish and crisp the zucchini, turn your broiler on high and finish roasting at a higher temperature for about 5 minutes.

While the zucchini is roasting, make the dressing: Combine all of the ingredients in a large bowl and whisk to blend, then set aside.

In the dressing bowl, toss the zucchini, red onion, tomatoes and beans. Once combined, add the feta cheese and serve.

TIP: Your broiler may be hotter or cooler, so it's important to watch the zucchini while it broils. Using the broiler helps to get more of a charred flavor on the vegetable, but you don't want it to burn.

SPICY BROCCOLI SALAD

I started making this dish using raw carrots instead of steamed broccoli, and that worked really well. But I think it works even better with broccoli. The dressing permeates through the broccoli's tree-like structure and holds on tight! Just be sure not to over-steam your florets; mushy broccoli will not hold up well against this thick and spicy dressing.

SERVES 4

BROCCOLI

2 cups (480 ml) water

6 cups (420 g) broccoli florets

2 tbsp (13 g) sliced scallion

Sesame seeds (optional)

DRESSING

2 tbsp (30 g) tahini

2 tbsp (30 ml) Sriracha

1 tbsp (15 ml) hoisin sauce

1 tbsp (15 ml) soy sauce

1 tbsp (15 ml) ponzu

To make the broccoli: Bring the water to a boil in a pot, then add the broccoli florets to a steamer basket and steam for about 5 minutes, or until the broccoli is bright green and tender yet still crisp.

While the broccoli is steaming, make the dressing: Combine all the ingredients in a bowl and mix well to combine.

Once the broccoli is cooked, drain it and add it to a large bowl. Toss the broccoli with half of the dressing and combine, adding more to your taste.

Serve warm, chilled or at room temperature, topped with the scallions and sesame seeds.

TIPS: I like to leave a bit of the bottom of the broccoli's stem on each floret for extra crunch.

Black or white sesame seeds would add an extra bit of texture and color to the dish.

VERY GREEN ISRAELI SALAD

I happen to love lettuce-less salads, and this one hits the spot, especially when it's served with other tasty bites. Israeli salads include traditional flavors of the Mediterranean diet: tangy lemon, fruity olive oil and deliciously ripe tomatoes. Small plates have become a great addition to menus across a wide swath of genres, and for good reason: Who wants to eat 50 bites of a large salad, when you can have 10 bites of five different kinds? At home, this type of dish works great when served as an easy appetizer with cocktails for a group, or alongside a protein for a simple meal. The big chunks of raw vegetables are healthy and satisfying—a duo that's not always easy to find!

SERVES 4

DRESSING
3 tbsp (45 ml) olive oil

Juice of 1 lemon

¼ tsp salt (or more to your taste)

SALAD
1 large or 2 medium green heirloom tomatoes

1 large green bell pepper

1 medium cucumber, peeled

¼ cup (25 g) sliced scallion

2 tbsp (1 g) chopped parsley

To make the dressing: In a small bowl or ramekin, whisk together the olive oil, lemon juice and salt.

To make the salad: Prepare your vegetables by slicing the tomatoes into half-moons, dicing the pepper into ¾-inch (2-cm) pieces, and removing the seeds and dicing the cucumber. Don't stress about the sizes. Try to cut the veggies into similarly sized pieces, but they will taste great no matter what the size. Uniformity is far more important when you are cooking things in order to ensure even doneness.

In a medium bowl, combine the tomatoes, pepper, cucumber, scallion and parsley, toss with the dressing and season to taste.

Serve alone, either cold or at room temperature, or with warm pita bread, hummus, hard-boiled eggs and olives.

TIP: The longer the vegetables sit in the dressing, the softer they will become—this isn't a bad thing, just a heads-up as it might not be to your taste.

CHILLED PEA SOUP WITH MINT AND GREEK YOGURT

There is something so refreshing yet so satisfying about a cold soup. I love the richness and sweetness of pea soup, but often it's made with ham, which I don't eat. This recipe is rich thanks to the hearty vegetable stock as well as the thick Greek yogurt. Paired with a piece of crusty bread or savory garlic bread, this is an easy meal. The hardest part is waiting for it to chill!

SERVES 4

1 tbsp (15 ml) olive oil

1 medium Vidalia onion, chopped

1 tbsp (14 g) butter

2 lbs (908 g) frozen peas

4 cups (946 ml) low-sodium vegetable stock, divided

¼ cup (15 g) chopped fresh mint

½ tsp salt

1 cup (226 g) low-fat plain Greek yogurt, divided

In a large saucepan, heat the olive oil over medium heat, then add the chopped onion and cook until golden brown, about 8 minutes.

Add the butter and peas and stir to coat. Add 3 cups (705 ml) of the stock, cover the saucepan and bring to a boil.

Once the stock comes to a boil, remove it from the heat, add the mint and transfer it to a blender or food processor. Blend until very smooth, then season to taste with salt; you may need more or less depending on your taste and the saltiness of your stock. Add ½ cup (113 g) of the Greek yogurt and reblend until just combined. If the soup is too thick, add the remaining 1 cup (235 ml) stock.

Place the soup into a glass container and chill in the refrigerator until it's cold. Serve cold with a dollop of the remaining Greek yogurt atop each bowl.

TIP: Frozen peas work wonders in many recipes, especially ones where the directions call for puréeing. Peas are widely available and incredibly inexpensive.

BROCCOLI AND PARMESAN SOUP

Growing up, I was always an adventurous eater, but I'm sure my mother still worried I wasn't eating enough vegetables. She is creative and a talented cook, and found ways to morph vegetables into more interesting versions of themselves. Working as her sous chef, my bubbe (grandmother) prepared everything before my mother came home from work. This soup is a take on a childhood dish and a family favorite—creamy broccoli soup with nutmeg. Nutmeg is often associated with sweet, baked goods, but it's so delicious with green vegetables, especially broccoli. I limit how much extra vegetable stock I use because I prefer really thick soups, but tailor the thickness of the soup to your tastes. Cooking the potatoes in the milk makes the soup so much richer without adding cream.

SERVES 4

---

2 heads broccoli

3 tbsp (45 ml) olive oil, divided

Salt to taste

1 cup (240 ml) whole milk

1 large russet potato, peeled and cut into 1" (2.5-cm) pieces

1 tbsp (14 g) butter

1 onion, thinly sliced

2 large cloves garlic, minced

½ cup (50 g) grated Parmesan cheese, plus more for garnish

¼ tsp ground nutmeg, plus more for garnish

1 ½ cups (355 ml) low-sodium vegetable stock, or more depending on how thick you like your soup

Preheat the oven to 425°F (220°C).

Remove the bottom portion of the broccoli stalks, and peel the thick outer layer with a vegetable peeler. Separate the florets from the bunch, and chop the stalks so that you are using the entire broccoli. Although the stalk is a bit fibrous for a salad, it is perfectly usable for this application.

Toss the broccoli with 2 tablespoons (30 ml) of the olive oil and salt to taste, spread on a baking sheet and roast until soft and golden brown, about 15 to 20 minutes.

Heat the milk in a large, heavy-bottomed pan over medium-low heat—you want to gently heat the milk so that it doesn't scald. Add the potato pieces to the milk and cook until tender, about 12 minutes. Once cooked, set the potato and milk mixture aside.

In a separate skillet, heat the remaining 1 tablespoon (15 ml) olive oil and the butter over medium heat, and cook the onion and garlic until translucent and fragrant, 8 to 10 minutes.

Place three-fourths of the onion mixture in a blender, and continue to cook the remaining portion until golden brown and more caramelized, another 10 to 12 minutes, then set aside for garnish.

Add the potatoes and milk, broccoli, Parmesan cheese and nutmeg to the blender or food processor with the onion, and blend until combined.

Begin adding the stock until you have achieved your desired consistency, adding more if you need. Season to taste with more salt if necessary.

Divide the soup among 4 bowls, top with a spoonful of the caramelized onions, a pinch of nutmeg and a sprinkle of Parmesan cheese. Serve immediately.

SEARED THAI EGGPLANT NAAN WITH TZATZIKI

Thai eggplants are small, round, green eggplants that are slightly bitter and studded with seeds inside. Eggplant lends itself well to many flavors, including the bold and tart flavors found in tzatziki. In our house, we like to eat this naan slathered with the cool and creamy tzatziki, but you should serve it any way you like.

SERVES 4

TZATZIKI

1 cup (227 g) low-fat plain Greek yogurt

2 hothouse cucumbers, peeled, seeded and grated either by hand or by using the grater attachment on your food processor

¼ cup (2 g) chopped dill

2 cloves garlic, very finely minced

¼ cup (60 ml) lemon juice

2 tbsp (30 ml) olive oil

Salt to taste

NAAN

Olive oil

8 small Thai eggplants, sliced into ½" (1.3-cm) rounds

4 cloves garlic, finely minced

2 prepared whole-wheat naan

Salt

Juice of ½ lemon

1 tsp chopped dill

To make the tzatziki: Place two wire-mesh strainers over two mixing bowls. Add the Greek yogurt to one strainer and the grated cucumber to the other, cover the strainers with paper towels, and let the yogurt and cucumber sit for at least 2 hours to drain. After at least 2 hours (and no more than 8 to 10), discard any liquid in the bowls. Combine the strained yogurt and cucumber with the dill, garlic, lemon juice and olive oil. Season to taste with salt and refrigerate.

Preheat the oven to 375°F (190°C).

To make the naan: Heat a large cast-iron skillet over medium heat. Once the skillet is hot, add enough olive oil to coat the bottom and add the sliced eggplant. Cook the eggplant for 3 to 4 minutes on each side, or until golden brown. If your oil is spitting, turn down the heat and cover the skillet.

While the eggplant cooks, mash the minced garlic into a paste using the flat side of the blade of a chef's knife.

Place aluminum foil or parchment paper over a baking sheet. Lightly brush the top of each naan with olive oil, and thinly spread the mashed garlic on top.

Tightly nestle the eggplant rounds onto the top of each naan. Lightly drizzle the top with olive oil, sprinkle with salt and bake for about 12 minutes, or until the naan is warmed through and the eggplant is further wilted.

Drizzle with the lemon juice, garnish with the dill and serve with the cold tzatziki.

TIP: Tzatziki will stay in the fridge for about 5 days. The flavor will intensify, so you may wish to make this dip the day before you are serving.

PERCIATELLI WITH BROCCOLI RABE AND ROASTED GARLIC CREAM SAUCE

I love serving this decadent meal in the cool fall and winter months with a glass of wine and a slice of crusty bread. Thick noodles work especially well here, as they are able to really grab hold of the rich sauce. Broccoli rabe adds a hearty freshness to a very rich dish. Although using whole roasted garlic cloves might seem aggressive, roasting brings out such a sweetness that it is not at all overpowering.

SERVES 4

SAUCE

1 head garlic, top quarter sliced off and discarded

1 tsp olive oil

4 tbsp (56 g) butter

3 tbsp (24 g) all-purpose flour

1 cup (240 ml) whole milk, or more to thin the sauce

¼ cup (25 g) shredded Parmesan cheese

¼ cup (62 g) ricotta cheese

½ tsp salt (optional)

1 bunch broccoli rabe, thick stem bottoms removed

Red pepper flakes (optional)

PASTA

1 tbsp (15 ml) olive oil

1 lb (454 g) thick pasta such as perciatelli

Preheat the oven to 375°F (190°C).

To make the sauce: Place the garlic on a piece of aluminum foil and drizzle with the olive oil. Wrap into a pouch and roast for 30 to 40 minutes, or until the garlic is soft and golden brown.

To make the pasta: Bring a large pot of salted water to a boil. Add the olive oil and then the pasta. Cook for 12 to 14 minutes for al dente pasta.

In a large saucepan, melt the butter over medium-low heat. When the butter is melted, add the flour and whisk well to combine. Be sure to heat the flour for at least 30 seconds to cook out the rawness.

Once the flour and butter have begun to thicken, add the milk a few small splashes at a time, whisking well after each addition. When the milk has been incorporated, add both cheeses and stir to combine. Remove each clove of garlic from the paper covering and add them to the warm cream sauce. Stir to combine. Season to taste with salt and reduce the heat to very low.

While the sauce is warming through, steam the broccoli rabe until it is tender but still crisp, about 5 minutes.

Drain the pasta and reserve at least ½ cup (120 ml) of the cooking liquid. Add the pasta to the garlic sauce and toss gently with tongs to distribute. If the sauce is too thick, add 1 tablespoon (15 ml) of the pasta cooking liquid at a time to thin it, then stir to combine. Add the broccoli rabe, stir again gently and serve immediately with red pepper flakes.

ASPARAGUS GALETTE WITH LEMON AND PARMESAN

Some flavors just work so well together, and asparagus, lemon and Parmesan are a few I love. The lemon in this dish really lightens the richer flavors of the buttery crust and salty cheese. If you aren't familiar with lemon zest, it adds a delicious brightness to dishes thanks to the rind's essential oils—just make sure you do not grate the white pith, which is very bitter.

SERVES 4

CRUST

1 ¼ cups (156 g) all-purpose flour

¾ tsp salt

½ cup (112 g) cold butter, cubed

5 tbsp (75 ml) cold water, or more as needed

ASPARAGUS

3 tbsp (45 ml) olive oil, plus more for drizzling

¾ cup (75 g) grated Parmesan cheese

1 bunch asparagus, woody stems removed

Zest and juice of 1 lemon

1 egg, beaten

To make the crust: Combine the flour and salt in a large bowl. Using a pastry cutter, work the butter into the flour until combined. Add the cold water, 1 tablespoon (15 ml) at a time, mixing well after each addition. If the dough won't come together, add more water, 1 tablespoon (15 ml) at a time. Wrap the dough in plastic wrap and refrigerate for at least 1 hour.

Once the dough has rested, roll it out on a floured workspace until it is about 10 inches (25.4 cm) in diameter. Place the dough on a nonstick silicone or parchment paper–lined baking sheet.

Preheat the oven to 375°F (190°C).

To make the asparagus: Combine the olive oil and Parmesan cheese in a bowl, then spread on the bottom of the crust, leaving 1 to 2 inches (2.5 to 5 cm) of room around the edges to fold the crust over the filling. Top the cheese mixture with the asparagus and drizzle the lemon juice on top. Fold the extra crust up over the asparagus as far as it will go. Drizzle additional olive oil over the top of the asparagus. Brush the crust with the beaten egg and bake for about 40 minutes, or until the crust is golden brown and flaky. Sprinkle with the fresh lemon zest and serve immediately.

TIP: Ricotta cheese would be an excellent substitute for Parmesan.

DOUBLE CHOCOLATE ZUCCHINI MUFFINS

Zucchini in a sweet muffin recipe?! Yes! I've always loved zucchini and banana breads, but really appreciate the convenience of muffins when I'm hosting guests. A touch of cinnamon adds a nice warmth to these muffins. It's so easy to bake a batch, serve them in a nicely lined basket with fresh butter, cream cheese or sweetened ricotta cheese, and call it brunch!

MAKES 12 MUFFINS

1 ¼ cups (156 g) all-purpose flour

3 tbsp (16 g) unsweetened cocoa powder

½ tsp salt

½ tsp baking powder

1 tsp ground cinnamon

2 eggs

½ cup (120 ml) melted coconut oil

1 tbsp (15 ml) vanilla extract

1 cup (202 g) granulated sugar

1 medium zucchini, shredded

½ cup (84 g) semisweet chocolate chips

Preheat the oven to 350°F (180°C). Grease a standard size nonstick muffin tin.

In a large bowl, combine the flour, cocoa, salt, baking powder and cinnamon.

In a medium bowl, whisk together the eggs, coconut oil, vanilla and sugar until well combined.

Add the shredded zucchini to the dry ingredients and stir well to coat the zucchini with the flour mixture. Add the egg mixture to the flour mixture and stir to combine, making sure there are no dry flour bits remaining. Fold in the chocolate chips and stir to combine.

Using an ice cream scoop, fill each muffin tin with batter approximately three-fourths of the way, being sure not to overfill. Bake the muffins for 20 to 25 minutes, or until a knife inserted into the center of a muffin comes out clean.

TIP: Using a good nonstick muffin tin is essential for baking muffins without paper liners. If you don't have a good nonstick option, use liners so that the muffins do not stick.

TOASTED PUMPKIN SEED, CUCUMBER AND AVOCADO SALAD

Buttery avocado and crispy cucumbers are perfect in this bright and delicious side dish. Toasted pumpkin seeds give an extra crunchy (and rich!) kick to a simple salad. Pair this salad with your favorite protein for a quick and easy, healthy and flavorful meal.

SERVES 4

DRESSING

2 tbsp (30 ml) olive oil

3 tbsp (45 ml) lime juice

½ tsp salt

SALAD

6 mini seedless cucumbers, sliced into ¼" (6-mm) coins

1 avocado, peeled, pitted and diced

¼ cup (29 g) pumpkin seeds

½ tsp red pepper flakes (optional)

To make the dressing: Combine all of the ingredients in a bowl and whisk to blend.

To make the salad: In a medium-size bowl, toss the cucumber with the dressing. Add the diced avocado and gently mix together; set aside.

Heat a skillet over medium-low heat. Add the pumpkin seeds and toast until they are warmed and fragrant, about 2 minutes. Remove from the heat and let cool slightly, then add the pumpkin seeds to the salad and toss to combine.

Top with the red pepper flakes, if desired, and serve at room temperature or refrigerate before serving.

TANGY GREEN BEAN AND POTATO SALAD

I am always amazed by how many potato salad varieties there are—heavy with mayonnaise or mustard, laced with hard-boiled eggs, simply prepared with salt and pepper—the list goes on and on. My take on potato salad is rich in flavor but still light thanks to the tangy and smoky vinaigrette, marinated onions and roasted green beans. I don't mean to brag, but my husband, who grew up avoiding potato salad at all costs, cannot get enough of this version.

SERVES 4

SALAD

10 oz (280 g) green beans, trimmed

1 tbsp (15 ml) olive oil

1 tsp salt, plus more for sprinkling

6 medium red bliss potatoes, halved

½ small red onion, thinly sliced

DRESSING

¼ cup (60 ml) olive oil

2 tbsp (30 ml) lemon juice

1 tsp ground cumin

½ tsp salt

Preheat the oven to 375°F (190°C).

To make the salad: Spread the green beans on a baking sheet, drizzle with the olive oil, sprinkle with salt and roast for 10 to 15 minutes, or until soft and golden brown.

Bring a large pot of water to a boil and add the 1 teaspoon salt. Once the water comes to a boil, add the potatoes, cover and cook for about 10 to 12 minutes, or until tender. Drain the potatoes.

To make the dressing: Whisk all of the ingredients together in a small bowl. Add the onion to the bowl and let marinate.

In a large bowl, gently toss the potatoes, marinated onions and roasted green beans. Serve warm, or room temperature.

ANCIENT GRAINS

Many people are familiar with the ancient grain quinoa—it's often touted as one of the healthiest grains because it is rich in protein and fiber. Rightfully so, it takes a prominent place in this chapter from the start of the meal to the end: appetizer to dessert. But there's more to ancient grains than just quinoa. Kaniwa, freekeh and wheat berries are three other examples of seldom-used but versatile, nutritious and delicious options. I hope that once you start stocking these goodies in your pantry, you experiment with them in conjunction with, or instead of, other grains and starches with which you may be more familiar. Farro is another one of my favorites, and it can easily be treated like rice and cooked using similar techniques. If you're looking for a risotto-like recipe that doesn't include rice, look no further than my Toasted Wheat Berries with White Beans, Burst Tomatoes and Parmesan (page 106) or my Marsala Mushroom Farro Risotto (page 110), two insanely delicious meals.

QUINOA AND KALE FALAFEL

Falafel is a traditional Middle Eastern specialty that's made from mashed chickpeas. There is no shortage of amazing falafel in New York City, from brick-and-mortar restaurants to food trucks. Traditionally, falafel is almost always fried, but my version is baked yet still mimics many of the flavors of the falafels you're accustomed to enjoying. And, this version comes packed with good-for-you quinoa, which helps bind and bulk the falafel. I like to serve these alone with a dip, or over crisp salad greens with olives, feta cheese, onions, lemon tahini dressing and a little hot sauce to keep things interesting.

SERVES 4

½ cup (85 g) quinoa

1 cup (240 ml) water

1 small onion, roughly chopped

2 cloves garlic

1 can (15 oz [420 g]) chickpeas, rinsed and drained

½ cup (34 g) chopped kale

¼ cup (15 g) chopped parsley

2 tbsp (30 ml) lemon juice

2 tbsp (30 g) tahini paste

2 eggs, beaten

1 tsp ground cumin

¾ tsp salt

2 tbsp (30 ml) olive oil, plus more as needed

In a small pot, bring the quinoa and water to a boil, then reduce the heat to low, cover and cook until the grain is soft but not mushy, 10 to 15 minutes. Set aside.

In a food processor or blender, pulse the onion, garlic and chickpeas until roughly chopped, and place in a bowl.

Add the kale and parsley to the food processor or blender, pulse to finely chop, and add to the chickpea mixture. Add the cooked quinoa, lemon juice, tahini paste, beaten eggs, cumin and salt to the chickpea mixture, stir to blend and refrigerate.

Preheat the oven to 425°F (220°C).

Once the oven comes to temperature, heat the olive oil in a large cast-iron skillet or oven-safe pan. Form the falafel by using an ice cream scoop and gently place each falafel in the hot oil. Cook on each side for 2 minutes, then brush the tops of each falafel with extra olive oil and place the entire skillet in the oven to bake for 18 to 20 minutes, or until the falafel are golden brown and crispy.

Serve the warm falafel over a salad, in a pita or on a bun.

TIP: This recipe is gluten free—perfect for dinner party guests who avoid wheat!

QUINOA SALAD WITH MINT, ZUCCHINI CHIPS AND WALNUTS

This salad bursts with spring flavors. These ingredients are especially in season during the spring, but are also available year-round. I almost always prefer bright and acidic flavors, which is why you might notice a different ratio of lemon juice to olive oil here. Especially against a simple backdrop such as quinoa, it works especially well. I love the different flavors, colors and textures of this dish.

SERVES 4

DRESSING

2 tbsp (30 ml) olive oil

3 tbsp (45 ml) lemon juice

¼ tsp salt

SALAD

¾ cup (128 g) quinoa

1 ½ cups (360 ml) water

1 tbsp (15 ml) olive oil

2 medium zucchini, thinly sliced into rounds

1 cup (144 g) peas

½ cup (63 g) shelled walnuts

Salt to taste

¼ cup (15 g) julienned mint

To make the dressing: Combine all of the ingredients and set aside.

To make the salad: In a small pot, bring the quinoa and water to a boil, then reduce the heat to low, cover and cook until the grain is soft but not mushy, 10 to 15 minutes. Set aside.

While the quinoa cooks, heat the olive oil in a large skillet over high heat. When the oil begins to shimmer, turn down the heat to medium and add the zucchini in one layer. Do not crowd the zucchini—cook them in multiple batches if you need to make sure they can caramelize, rather than steam. Cook for 4 minutes on each side, covered, then set aside.

With 3 minutes left on the quinoa, add the peas to the pot and warm through. When all of the water has evaporated, add the dressing to the warm quinoa and set aside.

In the same skillet in which the zucchini cooked, toast the walnuts over low heat until warmed and fragrant, 3 to 5 minutes.

In a large bowl, combine the zucchini chips with the quinoa mixture and toasted walnuts. Season to taste with salt. Top with the mint and serve immediately.

TIP: I like to nestle the zucchini chips by randomly placing them throughout the quinoa, but tossing them together works just as well.

WHEAT BERRIES WITH SAUTÉED MUSHROOMS AND GARLIC SCAPE PESTO

A couple of years ago, I excitedly opened my crop-share in July to find a green vegetable that looked like a cross between a scallion and a Chinese long bean. It turns out that I was fortunate to be exposed to garlic scapes. In season for a short time in the summer, garlic scapes, while delicious, are not for the wary—they are garlicky! But so good. They are the green shoot that sprouts up from the white garlic bulb while it grows. This salad packs a savory punch from the richness of the garlic scapes and the meatiness of the mushrooms. The pesto is thick and creamy and also works nicely as a dip.

SERVES 4

PESTO

¾ cup (50 g) sliced garlic scapes

½ cup (120 ml) olive oil

½ cup (50 g) shredded Parmesan cheese

¼ cup (60 ml) lemon juice

½ cup (60 g) walnuts

½ tsp salt

WHEAT BERRIES

2 cups (400 g) wheat berries, soaked in water to cover for at least 30 minutes and drained

4 cups (960 ml) water

2 tbsp (30 ml) olive oil

10 oz (280 g) mushrooms, cleaned and quartered

To make the pesto: Combine all of the ingredients in a blender or food processor and process until smooth. Set aside.

To make the wheat berries: In a pot, bring the wheat berries and water to a boil, cover and cook until tender, 35 to 40 minutes.

Heat the olive oil in a heavy-bottomed pan, then add the mushrooms and cook in one layer until sautéed and soft, about 8 minutes, flipping halfway through. If your pan is not big enough, cook the mushrooms in batches so that there is no overcrowding.

Once the wheat berries are cooked, place them in a large bowl. Add half of the garlic scape pesto and toss to coat. Taste the mixture and add more pesto to your liking. Add the mushrooms and gently toss to combine. Serve warm or at room temperature.

SUMMER CORN PESTO SALAD
WITH WHEAT BERRIES AND ARUGULA

Who doesn't love summer corn? Farm fresh, incredibly affordable and sweet as can be! I've even made this salad in the spring, when corn is not nearly as abundant or delicious, but still accessible. If you don't have fresh ears of corn on hand, you can certainly use frozen kernels. This is a great salad to serve at a BBQ—simple, easy to prepare and bursting with summery flavors and colors. I love using heirloom tomatoes because the colors are so vibrant and rich, but really any summer tomato should be well hued and will contrast nicely with the other colors in this salad.

SERVES 4

PESTO

1 bunch basil

¼ cup (25 g) grated Parmesan cheese

¼ cup (35 g) pine nuts, toasted

1 clove garlic, roughly chopped

¼ cup (60 ml) olive oil

¼ cup (60 ml) lemon juice

SALAD

1 cup (200 g) wheat berries, soaked in water to cover overnight and drained

2 cups (480 ml) water

1 cup (141 g) cooked corn kernels

4 small tomatoes, quartered

5 oz (144 g) arugula

2 scallions, thinly sliced

Salt to taste

To make the pesto: Combine all of the ingredients in a blender or food processor and process until smooth. Set aside.

To make the salad: In a pot, bring the wheat berries and water to a boil, cover and cook until they are soft but still have a bite to them, about 25 minutes. Set aside to cool.

In a large bowl, combine the wheat berries, corn, tomatoes, arugula and scallions, toss with 3 tablespoons (45 g) of pesto (or more to your liking), season with salt and serve immediately.

TIP: If you don't have enough time to soak overnight, just soak for 30 minutes. You'll need to cook them longer, but it eliminates the overnight step.

BARLEY SALAD WITH ROASTED GREEN BEANS, RADISH AND HAZELNUTS

Roasting green beans is my favorite way to enjoy this vegetable—it really brings out the flavor and is so much more interesting than steaming! Rumor has it that there was a two- to three-month period a few years ago that I ate roasted green beans for dinner in some capacity four or five days a week. What can I say: Tasty is tasty. This recipe takes the roasted beans to the next level, combining them with various textures: crunchy, crispy, smooth and soft!

SERVES 4

½ cup (100 g) pearl barley

2 cups (480 ml) water

10 oz (280 g) green beans, stems removed

2 tsp (10 ml) olive oil, divided

¼ cup (34 g) hazelnuts

¼ cup (10 g) very thinly julienned radish

1 tsp red wine vinegar

Salt to taste

1 avocado, peeled, pitted and thinly sliced

Preheat the oven to 425°F (220°C).

In a pot, bring the barley and water to a boil, then reduce the heat to low, cover and cook for 18 to 20 minutes, or until the water has evaporated and the grain is soft. Set it aside to cool.

While the barley cooks, toss the green beans in 1 teaspoon of the olive oil, spread on a baking sheet and roast for 12 to 15 minutes, or until the beans are golden brown and beginning to shrivel. With about 2 minutes remaining on the green beans, add the hazelnuts to the baking sheet and allow them to toast.

In a large bowl, combine the cooked and cooled barley with the radish, the roasted green beans and hazelnuts, the remaining 1 teaspoon olive oil and the red wine vinegar, and stir to combine. Season to taste with salt and top with the sliced avocado.

Serve at room temperature or refrigerate and serve cold. If you are serving this as a cold salad, wait until you are ready to serve to top with avocado—if you top it too early, it will brown.

*See photo on page 92.

TIP: If you are confident in your knife skills, you should have no problem slicing your radish very thinly. However, if you are uncomfortable doing this by hand, using a mandoline or the slicing attachment on your food processor will make this very manageable.

FARRO SALAD WITH ROASTED SWEET POTATOES, BRUSSELS SPROUTS AND HAZELNUTS

This salad is hearty and oh so delicious, on its own or served alongside other dishes. The hazelnuts are buttery and perfectly crunchy against the vegetables and farro. I especially love sweet potatoes when they're mixed with grains—there is just something so sweetly satisfying about a roasted sweet potato! My heaven.

SERVES 4

FARRO SALAD

1 large sweet potato, peeled and diced into bite-size pieces

2 tbsp (30 ml) olive oil, divided

4 cups (960 ml) water, divided

2 cups (176 g) halved or quartered Brussels sprouts, stems discarded

¾ cup (158 g) farro, soaked in water to cover for at least 30 minutes and drained

1 tbsp (14 g) butter

¼ cup (29 g) halved or crushed hazelnuts

DRESSING

¼ cup (60 ml) olive oil

2 tbsp (30 ml) honey mustard

1 tbsp (15 ml) apple cider vinegar

¼ tsp salt, plus more to taste

Preheat the oven to 375°F (190°C).

To make the salad: In a bowl, toss the diced sweet potato with 1 tablespoon (15 ml) of the olive oil, spread on a baking sheet and roast until soft, 30 to 40 minutes.

In a pot, bring 2 cups (480 ml) of the water to a boil and cook the Brussels sprouts for about 3 minutes, or until they are bright green and tender. Drain and set aside.

In a pot, bring the remaining 2 cups (480 ml) water and the farro to a boil, cover and cook until soft with most of the cooking liquid evaporated, about 25 minutes.

In a large skillet, melt the butter and the remaining 1 tablespoon (15 ml) olive oil. Add the Brussels sprouts and cook until golden brown without moving them for about 4 minutes so that they can caramelize in the pan. Toss and continue to cook until evenly golden; set aside.

To make the dressing: Combine all the ingredients in a bowl and mix well.

In a large bowl, toss the farro, sweet potatoes and Brussels sprouts with the dressing. Season to taste with additional salt if needed.

Toast the hazelnuts over low heat in a dry skillet until golden brown and warmed through, about 3 minutes. Top the salad with the hazelnuts and serve.

TIP: This salad is perfect when served immediately or after it has been made ahead. If you'd like to make this ahead, wait to toast the hazelnuts until you are about to serve the dish for the freshest flavor and best texture.

LEMON HERB BARLEY SALAD WITH FAVA BEANS

I'm one of those people who finds cooking incredibly therapeutic. What tops the list of my favorite mise-en-place tasks? Peeling carrots and shelling fava beans. I feel like I can accomplish so much in a short amount of time. It's totally mindless, but affords a real sense of accomplishment when the job is done. Looking down at my bowl of shelled fava beans totally gets my motor going. They are deliciously buttery, and pair so well with this recipe's tangy herb dressing.

"Mise-en-place" is a French cooking terms that means "everything in its place." It refers to the traditional culinary discipline of preparing, measuring and chopping all ingredients before you start actually cooking. It may sound like a pain, but if you take the time to prepare, things actually go smoother and quicker. I didn't believe it either, until I tried it.

SERVES 4

BARLEY SALAD
½ cup (100 g) pearl barley

3 cups (705 ml) water, divided

1 cup (126 g) shelled fava beans

HERB DRESSING
3 tbsp (45 ml) olive oil

2 tbsp (30 ml) lemon juice

2 cloves garlic, minced or crushed

½ tsp salt, plus more as needed

¼ cup (15 g) chopped mint

¼ cup (15 g) chopped parsley

¼ cup (15 g) chopped dill

To make the barley: In a pot, bring the barley and 2 cups (480 ml) of the water to a boil, then reduce the heat to low, cover and cook for about 20 minutes, or until the water has evaporated and the grain is soft. Set aside to cool.

In a separate pot, bring the remaining 1 cup (240 ml) water to a boil, add the fava beans and cook for 5 to 8 minutes, until bright green under their coating and tender when pricked with a knife, then drain and immediately plunge into a bowl of cold water; set aside to cool. Once the beans are cool, gently remove their outer skin by pressing them between your fingers or running the tip of a paring knife down the side and sliding the skin off.

To make the dressing: Place the olive oil, lemon juice, garlic, salt and herbs in a blender or food processor and blend to combine; set aside.

In a large bowl, combine the cooked and cooled barley with the fava beans and herb dressing, stirring gently. Season to taste with salt if needed and serve at room temperature or refrigerate and serve cold.

TIP: If you can't find fava beans, edamame or peas would work well in their place.

WINTER FARRO VEGETABLE SOUP

While traditional vegetable soups such as minestrone can contain pasta, I prefer an all bean and grain version. This soup is packed with vegetables and a heavenly rich tomato taste from both tomato paste and diced fresh tomatoes. If you're looking for a freezer-friendly meal for you or a friend, this is an easy, healthy and delicious option.

SERVES 4

2 tbsp (30 ml) olive oil

1 medium white onion, chopped

2 cloves garlic, chopped

1 cup (128 g) sliced carrots

1 cup (70 g) sliced mushrooms

¾ cup (158 g) farro

1 tsp dried oregano

2 tsp (3 g) dried basil

¼ cup (60 g) tomato paste

1 cup (160 g) seeded diced tomatoes

4 cups (946 ml) low-sodium vegetable stock

1 cup (250 g) white beans

1 cup (144 g) peas

1 cup (165 g) corn

2 cups (480 ml) water (optional)

Salt to taste

¼ cup (12 g) chopped chives

½ cup (50 g) grated Parmesan cheese

In a large saucepan, heat the olive oil over medium heat, then add the onion and cook until soft and translucent, about 5 minutes. Add the garlic and cook for 2 minutes longer.

Add the carrots and mushrooms and cook until golden brown, about 5 minutes. Add the farro, oregano, basil and tomato paste and stir to coat. Cook for 5 minutes, until the farro begins to toast.

Add the diced tomatoes and vegetable stock, turn up the heat and bring to a boil and cook, covered, for 20 to 25 minutes.

Add the white beans, peas and corn and cook for 10 minutes. If the soup is too thick for your liking, add up to 2 cups (480 ml) of water and continue cooking until it reaches your desired consistency.

Season to taste with salt and serve hot, topped with the fresh chives and Parmesan cheese.

TIP: If you cannot find good fresh tomatoes, you can substitute canned diced tomatoes—just be sure to adjust your salt accordingly as canned items can be salty.

TOASTED WHEAT BERRIES WITH WHITE BEANS, BURST TOMATOES AND PARMESAN

This is a deliciously comforting dish that works well year-round. Of course tomatoes are at their prime in the summer, but it's reasonably easy to find delicious tomato options throughout the year. I like to use a medley of various types of tomatoes for more color, but use whatever you have. Adding beans to this dish really bulks it up and helps to round out the flavors. Because this dish doesn't require the same attention as risotto, yet has an equally creamy texture, it's ideal for a dinner party dish—enjoy your company while the farro cooks, then slip away to the kitchen right before service and put the finishing touches on your meal!

SERVES 4

1 medium onion, thinly sliced

1 tbsp (15 ml) olive oil

2 tbsp (30 g) tomato paste

3 or 4 cloves garlic, minced

1 ½ cups (278 g) wheat berries, soaked in water to cover for at least 1 hour and drained

4 cups (960 ml) water or low-sodium vegetable stock, divided

½ cup (120 ml) dry white wine or full-bodied red wine

1 pint (298 g) cherry tomatoes, half halved and half whole

½ cup (125 g) canned navy beans or cannellini beans, rinsed and drained

½ cup (75 g) grated Parmesan cheese, divided, plus more for garnish

Salt to taste

Fresh parsley, for garnish (dried is okay if that's all you have)

In a medium heavy-bottomed pot, sauté the onion in the olive oil over medium-low heat until just wilted. Add the tomato paste and garlic, then stir to combine and cook for 2 minutes.

Add the wheat berries, stir to coat with the tomato paste mixture and let the grains toast for about 2 minutes.

Turn the heat up to medium-high, add 1 cup (240 ml) of the stock and the wine, stir to combine, then let simmer, stirring occasionally, until the liquid has evaporated, about 15 minutes.

Add the tomatoes and the remaining 3 cups (710 ml) stock, 1 cup (240 ml) at a time, and cook, stirring occasionally, until the liquid has evaporated, 10 to 15 minutes per cup (240 ml). Partially cover the pot with a lid.

When the last batch of stock is almost evaporated, add the beans and ¼ cup (38 g) of the Parmesan cheese, then stir to combine.

When all of the stock has evaporated, stir in the remaining ¼ cup (38 g) Parmesan cheese, season to taste with salt and serve immediately topped with a light dusting of Parmesan cheese and parsley.

TIPS: Soaking the wheat berries helps to cut the grain's cooking time, an added bonus for busy weeknights!

Rinsing canned beans helps remove almost half of the added sodium, so be sure to rinse well.

CRUNCHY QUINOA, GOAT CHEESE AND PISTACHIO-STUFFED ACORN SQUASH

In our house, we eat squash all year-round, and for some reason, guests are always surprised that it is part of the spread for a non-Thanksgiving meal. Stuffing may be a holiday treat we seldom enjoy during the rest of the year, but squash is a delicious and healthy vehicle in which to serve so many tasty foods. I really love the combination of the tangy pistachio stuffing with the natural sweetness of the acorn squash, plus an edible bowl makes cleanup that much easier.

SERVES 4

SQUASH

2 medium acorn squashes, halved vertically, seeds removed and reserved

1 tbsp plus 1 tsp (20 ml) olive oil

Salt to taste

PISTACHIO STUFFING

¾ cup (128 g) quinoa

2 tbsp (30 ml) olive oil, divided

1 ½ cups (360 ml) water

½ cup (29 g) acorn squash seeds

Salt to taste

¾ cup (110 g) shelled pistachios, skins removed as best as possible, divided

¾ cup (113 g) crumbled goat cheese

SCALLION VINAIGRETTE

1 bunch scallions, white and green parts finely chopped, divided

2 tbsp (30 ml) olive oil

¼ cup (60 ml) lemon juice

¼ tsp salt

Preheat the oven to 400°F (200°C).

To make the squash: Rub each squash half with 1 teaspoon of olive oil, season with a light sprinkling of salt, place on a sheet pan cut-side up and roast for 15 minutes. Flip them cut-side down, and roast for 20 minutes longer, or until the squash flesh is soft.

To make the stuffing: In a saucepan, mix the quinoa with 1 tablespoon (15 ml) of the olive oil and toast over medium heat until the grains begin to make popping sounds and turn a light golden brown, about 3 minutes. Add the water and bring to a boil, then reduce the heat to low, cover and cook until the grain is soft but not mushy, 10 to 15 minutes. Set aside.

While the quinoa is cooking, make the dressing: Combine three-fourths of the scallions with the other dressing ingredients, then set aside.

With about 10 minutes remaining on the acorn squash, toss the squash seeds with the remaining 1 tablespoon (15 ml) olive oil and a pinch of salt. Roast the seeds on the same sheet pan as the squash until golden brown, about 10 minutes.

Combine the cooked quinoa with three-fourths of the pistachios, goat cheese and scallion vinaigrette. Season to taste with salt. When the squash are finished roasting, fill each cavity with the pistachio stuffing, and garnish with the remaining pistachios, remaining scallions and toasted squash seeds. Serve immediately.

TIP: Pistachios can be skinned by rubbing them in the palms of your hands until most of the skin is removed. Leaving some skin on is fine, and adds color to the dish.

MARSALA MUSHROOM FARRO RISOTTO

Marsala wine is a fortified cooking wine and for this recipe I always opt for dry Marsala, which complements the meaty texture and umami flavor of cremini mushrooms. Trust me, I've tried both sweet and dry; dry is much better! Farro is a healthy whole-grain swap for traditional Arborio rice, and I bet if you don't share this secret ingredient with your guests, they would never know. Another plus for novice cooks is that while traditional risotto can be less forgiving, the sturdy farro hull affords you some wiggle room.

SERVES 4

MARSALA MUSHROOMS

1 tbsp (15 ml) olive oil

4 ½ cups (315 g) sliced cremini mushroom caps, wiped with a damp paper towel

1 medium Vidalia onion, thinly sliced

2 tbsp (28 g) salted butter

½ cup (120 ml) dry Marsala wine

¼ tsp salt

RISOTTO

1 quart (946 ml) vegetable broth

1 tbsp (15 ml) olive oil

1 ½ cups (278 g) farro, soaked in water to cover for at least 1 hour and drained

1 tsp chopped fresh thyme, plus more for garnish

4 tbsp (56 g) salted butter

½ cup (50 g) shredded Parmesan cheese

¼ tsp salt (optional)

1 tbsp (3 g) chopped chives, for garnish (optional)

To make the mushrooms: In a large heavy-bottomed pot, heat the olive oil over medium heat and cook the mushrooms until they are beginning to brown, about 5 minutes.

Add the onion, butter, Marsala wine and salt to the mushrooms, and stir to combine. Continue to heat the mushroom mixture until the alcohol in the Marsala wine is cooked off, about 8 minutes. Remove the mushrooms from the pot and set aside; because moisture leeches out of the mushrooms during cooking, there will still be some liquid in the pan after the alcohol has evaporated.

To make the risotto: Heat the vegetable broth in a pot over low heat until warmed through, about 5 minutes; keep warm.

Heat the same pot you cooked the mushrooms in over medium-low heat, add the olive oil, farro and thyme, and stir to coat the farro grains in the oil.

Add ½ cup (120 ml) of the warm broth to the farro, stirring constantly until absorbed. Repeat until all of the broth is incorporated into the farro, 30 to 45 minutes.

When the last portion of broth is absorbed into the farro, taste the farro to be sure it's tender. If it's not, you can add warm water ¼ to ½ cup (60 to 120 ml) at a time and continue cooking.

Return the mushroom mixture to the pot, add the butter and cook until the farro is soft and the mixture creamy, about 10 minutes. As you cook the farro, it will release its starch to thicken the broth.

Add the Parmesan cheese, stir to combine and season to taste with salt. Serve warm with extra thyme or chives as a garnish.

SPICE-RUBBED EGGPLANT WITH QUINOA AND CHERRIES

This dish is accidentally vegan: the flavors come together without anything animal-based. This dish is perfect for a vegan or vegetarian dinner guest, yet meaty enough to satisfy the carnivores! Eggplant cooks down to a soft and silky, mild-tasting vehicle for so many big flavors. It is rich in fiber, which will keep you full long after you have scraped the last morsel off of your plate. The cumin-scented quinoa imparts a spicy warm base layer for the other smoky and bright flavors to build on.

SERVES 4

---

2 large eggplants, halved, tops left intact

SPICE RUB

4 tsp (8 g) ground cumin

2 tsp (4 g) smoked paprika

1 tsp chili powder

1 tsp salt

2 tbsp (30 ml) lemon juice

¼ cup (60 ml) olive oil

QUINOA

⅔ cup (140 g) uncooked quinoa

1⅓ cups (320 ml) water

⅓ cup (53 g) unsweetened dried cherries or raisins

⅓ cup (20 g) chopped parsley, divided

⅓ cup (33 g) thinly sliced scallion (white and green parts), divided

Salt to taste

2 tbsp (30 ml) olive oil

2 tbsp (30 ml) lemon juice

Preheat the oven to 400°F (200°C).

To make the eggplant: Place the eggplant halves cut-side up on a nonstick baking sheet. With a sharp knife, score the eggplant diagonally every ½ inch (1.3 cm), then run the knife down the center of the eggplant. Be sure to only score the flesh of the eggplant; do not pierce through the skin.

To make the rub: In a small bowl, combine all of the ingredients for the spice rub. Massage the spice mixture evenly across each of the eggplant halves, being sure to rub it into the flesh. Turn the eggplants cut-side down and roast for 45 to 50 minutes, or until very soft and cooked through.

To make the quinoa: Combine the quinoa and water in a pot and bring to a boil over high heat. Reduce the heat to low, cover and continue to cook until the water has evaporated and the quinoa is fluffy, 10 to 12 minutes.

Mix the cooked quinoa with the cherries or raisins and set aside.

When the eggplant is cooked, add half of the parsley and half of the scallions to the quinoa, stir to combine and season to taste with salt. Top each eggplant half with equal amounts of the quinoa mixture, then top with remaining parsley and scallion, drizzle with the olive oil and lemon juice and serve immediately.

VEGGIE BURGERS WITH FARRO, CUMIN AND HONEY MUSTARD

One frustration I have is that "veggie burgers" at restaurants often contain no veggies! Sometimes they are made up of only simple grains and breadcrumbs. But these are different! Packed with actual vegetables, spices, nuts and chunky farro, they are deliciously filling and crazy versatile. Please don't be intimidated by the long list of ingredients—this recipe is as easy as turning on your blender or food processor. Trust me, the hardest part is trying to keep your shirt clean as you are devouring these babies with ketchup, mustard and your favorite condiment.

SERVES 4

¼ cup (47 g) farro

1 cup (240 ml) water

1 can (15 oz [420 g]) chickpeas, rinsed and drained

1 small red onion, roughly chopped

3 tbsp (45 ml) olive oil, divided

½ tsp salt

½ tsp ground cumin

½ tsp smoked paprika

½ tsp garlic powder

2 large eggs

1 tbsp (15 ml) honey mustard

½ cup (64 g) chopped carrots

½ cup (46 g) broccoli florets

¼ cup (50 g) toasted walnuts

¼ cup (39 g) steamed and shelled edamame

½ cup (54 g) panko breadcrumbs

Combine the farro and water in a pot and bring to a boil over high heat. Cook until the grain is soft but still has a bite, about 30 minutes. Drain any remaining water and set aside in a large mixing bowl.

Preheat the oven to 350°F (180°C).

In a blender or food processor, combine the chickpeas, red onion, 1 tablespoon (15 ml) of the olive oil and the spices. Pulse until combined but still chunky. Add the eggs and honey mustard, then pulse to incorporate. Add the chickpea mixture to the cooked farro.

Add the carrots, broccoli and walnuts to the food processor and pulse until very roughly chopped and approximately the same size. Add this to the chickpea and farro mixture, then add the edamame and panko. Stir well to combine.

Grease a large oven-safe pan or skillet (such as cast-iron) with the remaining 2 tablespoons (30 ml) olive oil. Form the mixture into 4 equal-size patties and place them on the greased pan or skillet. Bake for 8 to 10 minutes on each side, flipping once.

Serve immediately alone or on a toasted bun with your favorite condiments, such as cheese, ketchup, mayonnaise, mustard or relish.

TIPS: If you like a spicy burger, adding red pepper flakes or tangy hot sauce would be delicious.

These veggie burgers freeze well—either raw or cooked—just be sure to wrap them individually.

FREEKEH GRAIN BOWL WITH WALNUT VINAIGRETTE AND A POACHED EGG

There's something so delicious about mixing raw and cooked foods. I don't know why I love it so much—maybe it's a texture thing, or maybe it's just refreshing to crunch some raw vegetables every now and then! I like to mix everything in this dish together, creating a lusciously creamy sauce from the walnut vinaigrette and the runny egg yolk. Freekeh is a deliciously nutty whole grain with a distinctive smell and taste. It works perfectly here, standing up nicely to the many flavors and textures in this dish. The pickled onions are a quick and easy condiment and a crowd-pleaser. Use them to spice up your next taco night or atop your veggie burger for a crisp, tangy bite.

SERVES 4

PICKLED ONIONS
1 red onion, thinly sliced

¼ cup (60 ml) red wine vinegar

¼ cup (60 ml) water

1 tsp salt

1 tsp sugar

BOWL
1 cup (233 g) freekeh

2 ½ cups (600 ml) water

1 bunch broccoli rabe, thick bottom stems discarded

3 cloves garlic, finely minced

3 tbsp (45 ml) olive oil, divided

4 eggs

1 red pepper, cored, seeded and thinly sliced

WALNUT VINAIGRETTE
2 tbsp (30 ml) red wine vinegar

2 tbsp (30 ml) Dijon mustard

¼ cup (60 ml) olive oil

¼ cup (32 g) chopped walnuts

Salt to taste

To make the pickled onions: Combine all of the ingredients in a bowl and set aside.

To make the bowl: In a pot, bring the freekeh and water to a boil, then reduce the heat to low, cover and cook for about 15 minutes, or until the water has evaporated and the grains are soft.

Cook the broccoli rabe by placing it in boiling water for 2 minutes. While it's cooking, heat the minced garlic in a skillet with 1 tablespoon (15 ml) of the olive oil. Transfer the broccoli rabe to the skillet and toss with the garlic oil to combine. Cook for 2 minutes, until the broccoli rabe is tender but not mushy, then set aside.

In the same skillet in which the broccoli rabe was cooked, heat the remaining 2 tablespoons (30 ml) olive oil. Crack the eggs and fry them until the whites are set and the yolks are a bit runny, about 4 minutes.

While the eggs are cooking, make the dressing: Whisk the red wine vinegar and mustard together in a bowl, then drizzle in the olive oil and whisk until well combined. Add the walnuts, and season to taste with salt.

Plate the grain bowls by spooning equal amounts of the freekeh into each bowl, then working around the sides of the bowl, add the sliced peppers, broccoli rabe and pickled onions. Place 1 fried egg between the freekeh and the pickled onions and drizzle the freekeh with the walnut vinaigrette. Serve immediately.

TIP: I like to use a wide and shallow bowl for this recipe.

EGGPLANT QUINOA MEATBALLS

Some call them "hoagies," others call them "grinders" and still others call them "heroes." In Boston, we call deli sandwiches on a long roll "subs," and my mom often made cheesy meatball subs for dinner. She had a special way of making tomato sauce, and cooked her meatballs in a slow cooker in that delicious gravy. An easy meal for a busy family! My meatballs are perfect for vegetarian guests, and use quinoa and walnuts as binders instead of traditional day-old bread. This recipe makes for an easy DIY meal bar—you can offer cooked pasta, salads and sliced baguettes for sliders, and guests can choose their favorite vehicle! Easy for you, delicious for them.

SERVES 4

1 large eggplant, diced into 1" to 2" (2.5 to 5 cm) cubes

5 tbsp (75 ml) olive oil, divided

1 tsp salt

¼ cup (32 g) chopped walnuts

½ cup (93 g) cooked red quinoa

1 egg

½ cup (40 g) shredded Parmesan cheese

1 tsp dried oregano

2 tsp (7 g) garlic powder

½ cup (54 g) panko breadcrumbs

Preheat the oven to 375°F (190°C).

Toss the eggplant with 3 tablespoons (45 ml) of the olive oil and spread in an even layer on a cookie sheet lined with aluminum foil. Season with the salt and roast until soft, about 25 minutes.

While the eggplant cooks, combine the walnuts, quinoa, egg, cheese, oregano and garlic powder in a bowl.

Once the eggplant is cooked, add it to a blender or food processor with the remaining 2 tablespoons (30 ml) olive oil and blend until the mixture is chopped but still chunky. Pulsing works especially well to make sure your mixture doesn't turn into a purée—you want there to be some texture. Be sure to leave the oven on.

Combine the eggplant with the quinoa and slowly add the panko until the mixture resembles ground meat—you may or may not need all of the panko, so add it in batches.

Line the same baking sheet you used to roast the eggplant with a nonstick mat and form meatballs using an ice cream scoop. The recipe should yield between 10 and 12 meatballs, depending on the size of your scoop.

Bake the meatballs for 20 to 25 minutes, or until they are golden brown. Serve as you would traditional meatballs with tomato sauce and Parmesan cheese over pasta, with vegetables or on crusty bread.

TIPS: I especially love pesto with these meatballs. Any pesto recipe from this book would be delicious.

Keeping the eggplant skins on adds extra fiber, texture and color to the meatballs. Using red quinoa more resembles traditional meatballs, but if you only have regular white quinoa, that will work fine, too.

SMOKY BBQ TOFU SALAD GRAIN BOWL WITH KANIWA

Kaniwa is a lesser known grain—not as popular or as fashionable as quinoa, farro or even wheat berries. It's similar to quinoa in shape but smaller in size and just as nutrient dense with protein. I love its dark hue. Combining this underutilized grain with my BBQ tofu is not only delicious but also a nutritional powerhouse: protein on protein.

Tofu is an amazingly versatile plant-based, lean protein—mellow in flavor and delicious both cooked and fresh from the container. Tofu takes on most any flavor added to it, and really pairs well with this homemade smoky BBQ sauce, among others. This sauce is a delicious spread for sandwiches, and is perfect on my veggie burgers (page 114).

SERVES 4

BBQ SAUCE

1 cup (240 g) ketchup

¾ cup (180 ml) water

¼ cup (60 ml) red wine vinegar

3 tbsp (38 g) sugar

1 tbsp (10 g) garlic powder

1 chipotle pepper in adobo

1 tbsp (15 ml) lime juice

BOWL

3 cups (720 ml) water

1 block (14 oz [392 g]) extra-firm tofu, drained and diced into cubes

1 cup (170 g) kaniwa

1 head iceberg lettuce, shredded

1 cup (165 g) corn kernels

1 medium cucumber, peeled every other strip

1 cup (149 g) cherry tomatoes

1 medium yellow bell pepper, cored, seeded and thinly sliced

½ cup (73 g) shelled peanuts

½ cup (120 g) low-fat Greek yogurt

2 tbsp (30 ml) lime juice

To make the BBQ sauce: Combine the ketchup, water, vinegar, sugar and garlic powder in a pot and bring the mixture to a boil, then turn the heat down as low as possible and let it cook for about 30 minutes, or until the sauce has thickened and reduced in volume by about half. In a blender or food processor, combine the BBQ sauce with the chipotle pepper and the lime juice. Set aside.

Preheat the oven to 400°F (200°C). Cover a baking sheet with aluminum foil.

To make the bowl: Bring the water to a boil in a pot.

Toss the cubed tofu with the BBQ sauce and place on baking sheet. Bake the tofu for 25 minutes, or until the tofu is hot and the BBQ sauce has deepened in color.

While the tofu bakes, add the kaniwa to the boiling water and cook for 10 minutes. Reduce the heat, cover and continue cooking for about 10 minutes longer, or until the grain has softened and no water remains in the pot. If your kaniwa soaks up more water than you anticipated before the grain is tender, just add a bit more and continue cooking.

Plate the BBQ tofu grain bowl by arranging the vegetables and peanuts around a plate or dish, alternating colors, starting with the lettuce. When the kaniwa and BBQ tofu are finished cooking, add both to the grain bowl.

Mix the Greek yogurt with the lime juice and drizzle over the warm BBQ tofu.

Serve immediately with any remaining BBQ sauce.

WHEAT BERRY SALAD WITH MINT AND CRANBERRIES

This salad literally bursts in your mouth! When the wheat berries are cooked properly, they still have a bit of a bite. The crunch of the scallions and chew of the cranberries creates a perfectly balanced texture that is both visually appealing and so tasty. I really love this dish, and the vinaigrette is one of my favorites—simple, thick and tangy. It coats each of the salad's components beautifully, and brings each ingredient together. I often make a big batch and serve myself small portions all week, especially when I'm in a pinch and need to throw together a quick lunch.

SERVES 4

SALAD

2 cups (480 ml) water

1 cup (200 g) wheat berries, soaked in water to cover at least 1 hour

3 scallions, finely chopped (green and white parts)

¼ cup (30 g) dried cranberries

3 tbsp (8 g) chiffonade mint

VINAIGRETTE

2 tbsp (30 ml) olive oil

1 tbsp (15 ml) red wine vinegar

2 tbsp (30 ml) honey mustard

Salt to taste

To make the salad: Bring the water and wheat berries to a boil in a pot and cook until they are soft but still have a bite to them, about 25 minutes. Set aside to cool.

While the wheat berries are cooking, make the vinaigrette: Whisk all the ingredients together in a bowl and set aside.

In a large bowl, combine the wheat berries, scallions, cranberries and mint, toss with the vinaigrette, season to taste with salt and serve immediately.

TIP: To chiffonade your mint, lay each leaf one on top of another, roll the stack tightly and run a sharp, paring knife across the pile lengthwise, producing long and thin ribbons.

BLACKBERRY QUINOA SCONES WITH MAPLE GLAZE

There is something so lovely about baking on the weekends. In our house, we love to have leisurely weekend mornings, and baking is almost always on the agenda. For the record, "we" generally means "I bake, they eat." Whether I'm baking for a crowd (brunch guests!) or just my husband, it's quiet and peaceful and so delicious. Thanks to the addition of quinoa, these scones are hearty and sweet but not too sweet. Just right to start your Saturday or to occupy you in the kitchen while you listen to Sunday jazz—though there's nothing wrong with enjoying these any day of the week.

MAKES 8 SCONES

SCONES

2 ½ cups (300 g) all-purpose flour

2 tbsp (21 g) quinoa

1 tsp baking powder

½ tsp salt

½ cup (114 g) butter, cubed

½ cup (120 ml) whole milk

1 large egg

¼ cup (28 g) chopped pecans

1 cup (144 g) blackberries

GLAZE

¼ cup (60 ml) maple syrup

½ cup (69 g) confectioners' sugar

Preheat the oven to 375°F (190°C).

To make the scones: In a large mixing bowl, combine the flour, quinoa, baking powder and salt. Add the cubed butter and begin incorporating with a pastry cutter or a fork.

Whisk the milk, egg and pecans together in a small bowl. Pour the milk mixture into the dry ingredients and stir to combine. With your hands, mix the dough so that there are no dry spots remaining. Add the blackberries and fold into the dough with a spatula.

On a floured surface, form the dough into a disk shape, 1 to 1 ½ inches (2.5 to 3.8 cm) thick. With a serrated knife, slice the dough in half lengthwise, then in half horizontally. Slice each half in half so that you have 8 scones. Place on a nonstick silicone baking sheet and bake for 25 minutes.

While the scones are baking, make the glaze: Whisk together the maple syrup and confectioners' sugar in a bowl, then set aside.

When the scones are finished baking and still warm, use a fork to drizzle each with the maple glaze. Serve immediately.

TIP: Blackberries are deliciously tart, which nicely balances the sweet glaze, but any berry would do—blueberries, raspberries or even pitted cherries would be great.

PUMPKIN CRANBERRY AMARANTH MUFFINS

I'm a cook and a baker, and I love incorporating new flavors into familiar dishes. This recipe uses amaranth, a whole grain that's gluten-free, high in iron and zinc and a good source of protein. It looks similar to quinoa when it's both cooked and uncooked. Instead of using the entire grain in this recipe, I pulverized the amaranth before adding it to a more traditional muffin mixture. This recipe is almost vegan, and it could easily be made so by swapping the whole milk for soy or almond milk. Adding pumpkin purée is an easy way to bring sweetness, color and a bit of fiber to the muffins.

MAKES 12 MUFFINS

¼ cup (33 g) amaranth

1 ¾ cups (210 g) all-purpose flour

1 tsp baking powder

2 tsp (9 g) baking soda

¾ tsp salt

2 tsp (10 ml) vanilla extract

¾ cup (142 g) packed brown sugar

1 cup (240 ml) whole milk

⅓ cup (80 ml) melted coconut oil

½ cup (123 g) pure canned pumpkin

2 tsp (9 g) grated ginger

½ cup (61 g) dried cranberries

Sanding sugar, for garnish (optional)

Preheat the oven to 375°F (190°C). Grease the cups of a standard nonstick muffin tin very well.

In a spice or coffee grinder, pulse the raw amaranth grains until a flour forms.

In small bowl, combine the ground amaranth, flour, baking powder, baking soda and salt.

In a large bowl, combine the vanilla, brown sugar, milk, melted coconut oil, pumpkin, ginger and cranberries. Stir to combine.

Whisk the dry ingredients into the wet, making sure all the ingredients are well incorporated.

With an ice cream scoop or large spoon, fill each muffin cup three-quarters full, then sprinkle the top of each muffin with sanding sugar, if desired.

Bake for 20 minutes, and serve warm alone or with butter, cream cheese or jam.

TIP: If you're using an aerosol cooking spray to grease your muffin cups, try greasing the cups in the sink to avoid a messy situation.

STRAWBERRY CREAM AND SUGAR QUINOA BISCUITS

Adding quinoa to a baked good brings such an interesting texture to an already delicious recipe. In the summer, I often have such a bounty of strawberries that I am looking for alternatives uses for the fruit! Adding fresh berries creates a burst of sweetness and freshness, almost like cooking the jam right into the middle. But incorporating fresh fruit also means that the biscuits have to be enjoyed soon after they're cooked—they just don't keep very well. This really isn't a problem in my house, though. We seem to always find the right occasion to enjoy these goodies.

MAKES 12 BISCUITS

---

2 cups (240 g) all-purpose flour

¼ cup (43 g) uncooked quinoa

2 tsp (7 g) chia seeds

2 tsp (9 g) baking powder

½ cup (102 g) granulated sugar

½ tsp salt

4 tbsp (56 g) cold butter, cubed

1 ¼ cups (300 ml) light cream, divided

¾ cup (125 g) diced strawberries

1 egg, beaten

¼ cup (51 g) white sanding sugar

Preheat the oven to 400°F (200°C).

In a large mixing bowl, combine the flour, quinoa, chia seeds, baking powder, granulated sugar and salt. Add the cubed butter and begin incorporating with a pastry cutter or a fork. Pour in 1 cup (240 ml) of the light cream, reserving ¼ cup (60 ml) in case your dough doesn't need the extra liquid. Stir well to combine the wet and dry ingredients. If needed, add the remaining ¼ cup (60 ml) cream.

Fold in the diced strawberries. Using an ice scream scoop, place evenly sized biscuits on a silicone baking sheet or parchment paper–lined cookie sheet.

Brush each biscuit with the beaten egg, and generously sprinkle with white sanding sugar. Bake for 20 minutes, or until golden brown and a knife inserted into the center comes out clean. Serve warm.

TIP: Strawberries have a high water content, and will give off liquid as time passes, which can compromise the biscuits' texture. Be sure to enjoy these biscuits within a few days of making them.

FREEKEH TABBOULEH

My mother always keeps store-bought tabbouleh in the fridge. It wouldn't be a late-night Friday arrival at my parents' house for a weekend visit without a few midnight forkfuls. It is funny how you associate certain foods with random memories. Traditional tabbouleh is made with cracked wheat or bulgur. My version mimics many of the dish's traditional flavors, but uses freekeh as a nuttier whole-grain base. If you don't have freekeh on hand, using cracked wheat, bulgur or quinoa would work equally well.

SERVES 4

TABBOULEH

½ cup (117 g) freekeh, rinsed

2 cups (480 ml) water

¼ cup (15 g) chopped mint

¾ cup (45 g) chopped parsley

2 medium tomatoes on the vine, seeded and diced

2 hothouse cucumbers, peeled, seeded and diced

DRESSING

¼ cup (60 ml) olive oil, divided

¼ cup (60 ml) lemon juice

½ cup (80 g) chopped white onion

1 tsp salt, plus more as needed

To make the tabbouleh: Bring the freekeh and water to a boil in a pot, then reduce the heat to low, cover and cook for about 15 minutes, or until the water has evaporated and the grain is soft. Set aside to cool.

While the freekeh cooks, make the dressing: Combine the olive oil, lemon juice, onion and salt in a bowl. Whisk vigorously to combine and set aside.

In a large bowl, combine the cooked and cooled freekeh with the mint, parsley, tomatoes and cucumbers. Add the dressing and stir to combine. Season to taste with salt and serve at room temperature or refrigerate and serve cold.

TIPS: Freekeh can be made ahead of time and stored in the refrigerator for up to 3 days.

While untraditional, feta cheese would pair very well with this dish.

HERBED QUINOA SALAD WITH CHICKPEAS, FETA AND POMEGRANATE SEEDS

One thing I especially love about quinoa—besides its health benefits, its texture, its versatility in various applications, its forgiving nature to overcooking, its general availability (okay, so there are a lot of things I like about quinoa . . .)—is that it really takes on the flavors of what you mix with it. Talk about flexibility! Here, the strong flavors of the mint and feta cheese pair seamlessly with the sweetness of the pomegranate seeds and the tanginess of the dressing. I especially like to serve this as a side, along with other dishes, but it's so good I've been known to serve myself a large portion and call it a meal.

SERVES 4

QUINOA

1 cup (210 g) uncooked quinoa

2 cups (480 ml) water

⅓ cup (50 g) pomegranate seeds

⅓ cup (50 g) crumbled feta cheese

⅓ cup (20 g) julienned mint

¾ cup (169 g) chickpeas

DRESSING

⅓ cup (80 ml) olive oil

¼ cup (60 ml) lemon juice

2 tbsp (30 ml) red wine vinegar

1 clove garlic, very well minced or run through a garlic press

½ tsp salt, plus more as needed

To make the quinoa: In a medium-size pot, bring the quinoa and water to a boil. Reduce the heat to low, cover and cook until the grain is soft but not mushy, 10 to 15 minutes. Set aside to cool (if you add the feta to hot quinoa, it will melt and won't hold its shape against the grain).

To make the dressing: In a small bowl, whisk all of the ingredients together.

Add the dressing to the cooled quinoa, then fold in the pomegranate seeds, feta, mint and chickpeas. Season to taste with additional salt if needed. Serve immediately.

TIP: In my house, the leftovers (if there are any!) are often tossed with salad greens for a light lunch or simple dinner.

MODERN GRAINS

This chapter focuses on modern grains that you may be more familiar with, such as rice and corn. But just because they are ubiquitous does not mean that they are boring! Grains are excellent pantry staples: They have long shelf lives and are durable, economical, versatile and so delicious. In fact, we keep so many grains in our (modestly sized) New York City apartment kitchen that my husband often remarks that we could open a market.

With so many ways to use these grains, the possibilities are endless. I especially love elevating standard grains with big bursts of flavor, as in my Creamy Polenta with Smoked Gouda and Red Wine–Braised Mushrooms (page 136). I made this dish one evening for my aunt who was visiting from out of town and she loved it. I knew it had to be featured in this book. I hope you love it as much as we do!

CRISPY ZUCCHINI FRIES WITH LEMON YOGURT

If you've ever ordered zucchini fries from your local pizza place, you know how delicious they are. But because they are often fried, they can be heavy and oily. My version, coated with garlicky cornmeal and Parmesan cheese, is lighter, baked in the oven and just as tasty! Also, instead of pairing them with a rich marinara sauce that covers up the zucchini, I serve them with a refreshing lemon yogurt sauce.

SERVES 4

FRIES

½ cup (120 ml) whole milk

2 eggs

1 cup (122 g) medium-grain cornmeal

1 cup (100 g) Parmesan cheese

1 tsp salt

1 tsp garlic powder

½ tsp smoked paprika, plus more for garnish

4 medium zucchini, sliced in half and then quartered lengthwise

LEMON YOGURT

1 cup (240 g) low-fat Greek yogurt

¼ cup (60 ml) lemon juice

2 tbsp (30 ml) olive oil

Salt to taste

Preheat the oven to 375°F (190°C). Line a baking dish with aluminum foil and set aside.

To make the fries: In a bowl, whisk together the milk and eggs until combined.

In another bowl, combine the cornmeal, Parmesan cheese, salt, garlic powder and paprika.

With one hand reserved for wet and one hand reserved for dry, dredge each zucchini fry in egg, then coat in the seasoned cornmeal-Parmesan mixture. Place the zucchini fries on the aluminum foil, then sprinkle with paprika for extra color and flavor.

Bake the zucchini fries for 15 to 20 minutes, or until the coating is crisp and the insides of the vegetable are soft but not falling apart.

To make the lemon yogurt: Mix all the ingredients together, season to taste with salt and place in a small bowl or ramekin. Serve immediately with the fries.

PARMESAN AND PEA ARANCINI WITH CHUNKY TOMATO SAUCE

These arancini bites are a play on traditional Italian deep-fried rice balls. They are packed with cheesy rice and studded with delicious peas, and are meat free! Making your own tomato sauce is so simple, and really adds to the flavor of this dish. I like serving these as mini rice balls for appetizers, though you could easily make larger versions. I hope you aren't intimidated by the numerous steps in this recipe—I promise nothing is too complicated!

SERVES 4 TO 6

TOMATO SAUCE

1 tbsp (15 ml) olive oil

2 pints (600 g) cherry tomatoes, halved

¼ cup (60 ml) red wine

¼ cup (60 ml) water

½ tsp sugar

Salt to taste

ARANCINI

3 tbsp (45 ml) olive oil

1 onion, diced

4 cloves garlic, minced

1 cup (200 g) white rice

2 cups (480 ml) water, or more as needed

1 cup (134 g) peas

2 ½ cups (250 g) grated Parmesan cheese, divided

1 cup (113 g) shredded mozzarella cheese

1 tsp salt

3 eggs, divided

1 cup (122 g) coarse cornmeal

½ cup (60 g) fine cornmeal

2 tbsp (19 g) garlic powder

To make the tomato sauce: Heat the olive oil in a sauté pan over medium-high heat. Once the oil is hot, add the halved tomatoes and cook for 3 minutes. Add the red wine and water, bring to a boil, cover and cook for 6 minutes. Reduce the heat to medium-low, keep the tomatoes covered, and cook for 25 to 30 minutes. When the sauce is finished cooking, add the sugar and season to taste with salt. Place in a blender or food processor and pulse until the sauce is thinner in consistency but still chunky.

To make the arancini: In a large pot, heat the olive oil over medium heat. Add the onion and cook until translucent, about 5 minutes. Add the garlic and rice, then stir to coat the rice with the oil and onions.

Add the water, 1 cup (240 ml) at a time, stirring well after each addition. Don't add the next cup until most of the previous liquid has been absorbed. After all 2 cups (480 ml) of water have been absorbed, check the rice for doneness. If the rice needs more cooking time, add more water. Once the rice is finished, add the peas, 2 ¼ cups (225 g) of the Parmesan, the mozzarella and the salt and stir well to combine. Remove from the heat to slightly cool.

Preheat the oven to 375°F (190°C). In a large bowl, beat 1 of the eggs and stir into the rice mixture. While the rice continues to cool, assemble the two dredging stations by whisking the remaining 2 eggs in one bowl and combining both cornmeals, the garlic powder and the remaining ¼ cup (25 g) Parmesan cheese in another.

With an ice cream scoop, two spoons or your hands, form the rice into balls. Roll the arancini in the egg, then in the seasoned cornmeal and place on a parchment or silicone mat–lined baking sheet. Bake for 30 minutes, or until the cornmeal crust has hardened. Serve warm with the chunky tomato sauce.

SESAME, KALE AND RICE SALAD

I love grain-based salads, and rice works perfectly to balance the many textures in this dish. It can be served warm or cold, depending on how quickly after you toss the rice with the other ingredients. If you serve it warm, the rice begins to just wilt the kale, but when served cold it's crispy and refreshing. While this recipe is vegan, the savory, Asian-inspired flavors would be great paired with a protein such as chicken, salmon, tofu or my favorite—seared tuna.

SERVES 4

DRESSING

¼ cup (60 ml) toasted sesame oil

2 tbsp (30 ml) soy sauce

1 tbsp (15 ml) ponzu

1 tbsp (15 ml) seasoned rice vinegar

2 cloves garlic, chopped

1 tsp minced ginger

SALAD

2 cups (480 ml) water

½ cup (93 g) white rice

½ cup (83 g) corn kernels

¼ cup (26 g) shelled peanuts

1 bunch kale, thick center ribs discarded

2 tbsp (16 g) black sesame seeds, divided

¼ cup (25 g) sliced scallion, divided

To make the dressing: In a blender or food processor, combine all the dressing ingredients, pulse to combine and set aside.

To make the salad: In a large pot, bring the water to a boil, add the rice and cook for 15 minutes. Turn off the heat, add the corn to the rice, place a lid on the pot and let the rice and corn steam for at least 5 minutes. Fluff with a fork and set aside.

While the rice is cooking, toast the peanuts in a dry skillet over medium-low heat until warm, golden brown and fragrant, about 3 minutes.

In a large bowl, toss the kale with the sesame dressing. With very clean hands, rub the kale and dressing together until well combined and the kale glistens with an even coating of dressing.

Toss the kale with the rice and corn mixture, and half each of the sesame seeds, scallions and peanuts.

Serve family style or in individual bowls topped with the remaining sesame seeds, scallions and peanuts.

SMOKY CHILLED CORN AND ROASTED SWEET POTATO SOUP

We're big sweet potato fans in my family. They're packed with nutrition, so delicious and gorgeously hued. Luckily, in this soup, sweet potatoes and Greek yogurt offer the creaminess and thickness of heavy cream without the calories and fat. Adding a chipotle pepper imparts a slight bite but a strong smoky flavor that pairs so nicely with the cool sweet potatoes and the creamy Greek yogurt. I love the versatility of this soup— make it your own by adding your favorite toppings.

SERVES 4

1 large sweet potato, peeled and chopped

¼ cup (60 ml) olive oil, divided

1 medium red onion, chopped

2 cloves garlic, chopped

3 cups (495 g) corn kernels, divided

2 cups (480 ml) low-sodium vegetable stock, or more as needed, divided

1 chipotle pepper in adobo sauce

1 tsp paprika

½ cup (120 g) low-fat plain Greek yogurt

2 tsp (10 ml) lime juice

Salt to taste

¼ cup (12 g) chopped chives

Red pepper flakes (optional)

Preheat the oven to 400°F (200°C).

Coat the sweet potatoes with 2 tablespoons (30 ml) of the olive oil, spread on a baking sheet and roast for 25 minutes, or until they are fork tender.

While the potatoes cook, heat the remaining 2 tablespoons (30 ml) olive oil in a large stockpot. Add the onion and cook, covered, until translucent and tender, about 10 minutes. Then add the garlic and cook for another 2 minutes.

Add 2 cups (330 g) of corn, 1 cup (240 ml) of vegetable stock and the chipotle in adobo sauce to a food processor or blender and combine until very smooth and creamy.

Once the onions and garlic are cooked, add the remaining 1 cup (240 ml) vegetable stock and deglaze the pan by cooking for another 2 minutes. Be sure to scrape the goodness off the bottom with a wooden spoon. Add the cooked onions, garlic and sweet potatoes to the corn purée and blend until smooth.

Place half of the puréed soup into the same stockpot you used for the onions and garlic, add the remaining 1 cup (165 g) of corn and the paprika, and cook over low heat until the corn is cooked through, about 10 minutes.

Add the Greek yogurt and lime juice to the soup in the blender and combine until smooth, then add this mixture to the soup on the stove. Turn off the heat and stir to combine the two batches.

If the soup is too thick for your taste, add another 1 cup (240 ml) of vegetable stock, stir and let cool to room temperature before refrigerating. Season to taste with salt.

Serve the soup chilled, topped with the chopped chives and red pepper flakes, if desired.

CREAMY POLENTA WITH SMOKED GOUDA AND RED WINE–BRAISED MUSHROOMS

I first made this recipe on an unseasonably cold spring evening. My husband and I were looking for something warm and cozy, and this recipe popped into my head. I've cooked it many times over and we've been enjoying it ever since—primarily in the winter, when we are especially chilly and looking for a quick weeknight meal. It uses the richness of smoked Gouda to add that distinctive luxuriousness to the polenta. If you haven't had smoked Gouda, please put the book down and run (do not walk) to your grocery store. You can thank me later.

SERVES 4

POLENTA

4 cups (960 ml) whole milk

1 cup (240 ml) water

2 cups (244 g) medium-grain, quick-cooking polenta

2 cups (200 g) grated smoked Gouda cheese

2 tbsp (28 g) butter

Salt to taste

MUSHROOMS

4 tbsp (56 g) butter

2 tbsp (30 ml) olive oil

4 portobello mushrooms, wiped clean, stems discarded and tops thinly sliced

1 tsp dried thyme, plus more for garnish

1 tsp all-purpose flour

¾ cup (180 ml) full-bodied red wine such as Cabernet Sauvignon

To make the polenta: Combine the milk, water and polenta in a medium-size pot and bring to a boil. Be sure to stir well so there are no clumps. Cook for about 10 minutes, or until the liquid is absorbed and the polenta is soft and creamy. Add the Gouda cheese and stir to combine. Add the butter and stir to combine. Season to taste with salt.

To make the mushrooms: Melt the butter and olive oil in a large skillet over medium heat. Add the mushrooms, then cover and let cook for about 3 minutes. Add the thyme, flour and red wine and stir well to incorporate the flour. Re-cover and cook for 6 minutes, then turn the heat down as low as possible and keep warm until the polenta is finished.

Plate by spooning the polenta into a bowl and topping with the braised mushrooms and a sprinkling of additional thyme. Serve immediately.

*See photo on page 128.

TIPS: Any mushroom will work in this recipe, so use whatever you have. I happen to like the shape of sliced portobellos, but that's just personal preference.

This recipe is best enjoyed right after cooking. But, if you need to make it ahead of time, keep the polenta and mushrooms separate. When it's time to serve, reheat the polenta with additional milk to thin out the texture and make it creamy again. It might not ever come back to its original form, but it will be better than anything reheated in the microwave.

WHITE WINE, LEMON AND PARMESAN RISOTTO WITH ROASTED BRUSSELS SPROUTS

My husband and I are Brussels sprouts lovers. We almost always order them at restaurants and I make them frequently at home. I'm a firm believer that anything in the cabbage family should not be served boiled or steamed—these cruciferous vegetables really need some extra cooking time to caramelize and enhance their flavors. The Brussels sprouts are crunchy and deliciously roasted and balance the creaminess of the risotto. This dish is gorgeous to look at, with the green Brussels sprouts, yellow lemon zest and pink-flecked white rice. I love the slight pink hue the red onions give off as they cook, but if you prefer a whiter rice, swap the red onion for any white onion and dig in.

SERVES 4

RISOTTO

4 cups (940 ml) low-sodium vegetable stock

3 tbsp (42 g) butter

1 medium red onion, chopped

2 cloves garlic, chopped

2 tbsp (30 ml) olive oil

1 cup (240 ml) white wine

1 ¼ cups (250 g) Arborio rice

1 cup (100 g) shredded Parmesan cheese

Zest and juice of 1 lemon

Salt to taste

BRUSSELS SPROUTS

2 tbsp (28 g) butter

2 tbsp (30 ml) olive oil

9 oz (250 g) Brussels sprouts, stems removed and halved

To make the risotto: In a small saucepan, heat the vegetable stock over low heat to warm through.

Preheat the oven to 400°F (200°C).

In a large saucepan, melt the butter over medium heat, then add the chopped onion and cook until translucent, about 4 minutes. Add the garlic and cook for 2 minutes longer.

Add the olive oil, white wine and rice and stir to coat. Cook for 4 to 5 minutes, or until the rice has absorbed all of the wine.

Meanwhile, make the Brussels sprouts: Once the oven comes to temperature, add the butter and olive oil to a cast-iron or oven-safe skillet to melt. Add the Brussels sprouts, cut-side down, and roast until golden brown, 25 to 30 minutes.

Start adding the warmed stock, 1 cup (240 ml) at a time, to the rice, stirring constantly. Once each cup of stock has been absorbed, add another until the risotto is cooked and creamy, 30 to 35 minutes.

Add the Parmesan cheese and lemon juice, stirring well to combine. Season to taste with salt.

Plate the risotto and top with the roasted Brussels sprouts, then sprinkle with the lemon zest and a little more salt. Serve immediately.

POLENTA WITH PARMESAN AND RED WINE TOMATO RAGÙ

This recipe is especially great in the summer, when corn and tomatoes are at their peak, but it's easy enough to find these tasty ingredients year-round as well. I love the unexpected crunch of corn in the otherwise super creamy polenta, and the rustic appeal of the homemade chunky tomato ragù. Isn't there something so satisfying about a homemade sauce? If you're a meat eater, adding browned ground beef to the sauce would likely be delicious.

SERVES 4

POLENTA

4 cups (960 ml) whole milk

1 cup (240 ml) water

2 cups (244 g) medium-grain, quick-cooking polenta

1 ¾ cups (175 g) grated Parmesan cheese, plus more for garnish

3 tbsp (42 g) butter

1 cup (165 g) corn kernels

Salt to taste

TOMATO RAGÙ

4 tbsp (56 g) butter

2 tbsp (30 ml) olive oil

2 lbs (910 g) tomatoes on the vine, seeded and roughly diced

2 tsp (5 g) all-purpose flour

¾ cup (180 ml) full-bodied red wine such as Cabernet Sauvignon

To make the polenta: Combine the milk, water and polenta in a medium-size pot and bring to a boil. Be sure to stir well so there are no lumps. Cook for about 10 minutes, or until the liquid is absorbed and the polenta is soft and creamy. Add the Parmesan cheese, butter and corn, then stir to combine. Season to taste with salt.

While the polenta is cooking, make the ragù: Melt the butter and olive oil in a large skillet over medium heat. Add the tomatoes, then cover and let cook for about 2 minutes. Add the flour and red wine and then stir well to incorporate the flour. Re-cover and cook for 10 minutes, then turn the heat down as low as possible and keep warm until the polenta is finished.

Scoop the polenta into a bowl and top with the tomato ragù and additional Parmesan cheese, then serve immediately.

TIP: Polenta is best served very soft and creamy. The longer it sits, the more it will harden. I suggest making and then quickly serving this dish.

CRANBERRY CASHEW GRANOLA

I've been making granola at home for years—it's a great item to serve to brunch guests, and to have around the house for a quick meal or snack. It's also a great giftable item, one that I often give to hostesses and new moms. Traditionally, granola is soaked in sugar and oil, but my version is a bit lighter and truly delicious. The brown sugar, cinnamon and salt make for an especially well-balanced and tasty bite. If you aren't a cranberry or cashew fan, swap in your favorite dried fruit and nuts. This recipe lends itself very well to modification, so use what you have on hand and enjoy!

SERVES 8

1 egg white, beaten

2 tbsp (30 ml) water

3 cups (240 g) old-fashioned rolled oats

½ cup (95 g) packed brown sugar

½ cup (120 ml) melted coconut oil

2 tsp (10 ml) vanilla extract

1 tbsp (8 g) ground cinnamon

1 tsp salt

¼ cup (40 g) very roughly chopped cashews

⅓ cup (50 g) dried cranberries

Preheat the oven to 300°F (149°C).

In a large bowl, whisk together the egg white and water until foamy, then add the oats and toss to coat.

In a small bowl, whisk together the brown sugar, coconut oil, vanilla, cinnamon and salt, then pour into the oat mixture and toss well to combine.

Cover a rimmed baking sheet with a nonstick baking mat or parchment paper and spread the oat mixture in one even layer. This granola bakes best on metal trays—glass baking dishes do not work as well.

Bake for 20 minutes, then add the cashews and bake for 20 minutes longer, stirring occasionally.

After 40 minutes, turn the oven off and let the granola sit in the oven for an additional 10 minutes. Remove the granola from the oven, add the cranberries, toss to combine and allow to cool. Granola crisps up as it cools, so do not worry if yours doesn't seem hard enough fresh out of the oven.

Enjoy over yogurt, with milk or on its own.

TIP: Store granola unrefrigerated in a covered container for up to 1 week.

FORBIDDEN RICE SALAD WITH GOLDEN BEETS, GOLDEN RAISINS AND WALNUTS

This salad is bursting with textures and flavors! I love the chewiness of the raisins paired with the crunchiness of the walnuts and the al dente bite of the beets. Golden raisins and golden beets work particularly well in this recipe because their vibrant color is a stunning contrast to the rice's dark hue, while their natural sweetness complement and balance the tangy dressing. Dark raisins and beets, while still tasty, create a monochromatic dish. This salad gets better with time. Make a big batch and enjoy it over and over—warm or cold. And really, who doesn't like leftovers?

SERVES 4

DRESSING

2 tbsp (30 ml) olive oil

2 tbsp (30 ml) seasoned rice vinegar

2 tbsp (30 ml) lemon juice

½ tsp salt

RICE

1 cup (160 g) black or wild rice, rinsed

2 ¼ cups (530 ml) water

1 large golden beet, peeled and diced into bite-size pieces

2 tsp (10 ml) olive oil

¼ cup (30 g) walnuts

¼ cup (40 g) golden raisins

2 celery stalks, diced

2 scallions, thinly sliced

Preheat the oven to 375°F (190°C).

To make the dressing: In a bowl, whisk together the dressing ingredients and set aside.

To make the rice: In a heavy-bottomed pan, bring the rice and water to a boil, cover and reduce the heat to very low. Cook until the rice is soft but not overdone and the liquid is absorbed, about 35 minutes.

While the rice is cooking, toss the beets with the olive oil, spread on a baking sheet and roast until golden brown and soft, about 25 minutes.

In a pan over low heat, toast the walnuts for 3 to 5 minutes, or until golden and fragrant, let cool slightly and roughly chop.

Once the rice is cooked, immediately combine the raisins and warm rice in a large bowl, then add the walnuts, celery, scallions, beets and dressing. Stir to combine.

Serve warm or refrigerate for later use.

TIPS: Be mindful of black rice: It might stain a light-colored ceramic pot. You may have some success mitigating this by rinsing the rice beforehand.

Seasoned rice vinegar is sweeter than unseasoned rice vinegar—if you think you might prefer a more savory side dish, opt for the unseasoned variety.

ISRAELI COUSCOUS WITH SCALLIONS, CRANBERRIES AND CAPERS

While couscous is a fine semolina grain, Israeli couscous (also called pearl couscous) is much larger—about the size of peppercorns. Toasted couscous is kind of like the love child of brown rice and orzo. We eat with our eyes before our mouths, and this colorful dish will not disappoint. The neutral couscous allows the colorful fruits and vegetables to pop, in terms of both color and flavor. This dish is delicious—sweet and salty combinations are so satisfying!

SERVES 4

2 tbsp (30 ml) olive oil, divided

2 cups (300 g) Israeli couscous

2 ½ cups (600 ml) water

½ cup (61 g) dried cranberries

2 tbsp (17 g) capers, or more to taste

¼ cup (25 g) sliced scallion, divided

Salt to taste

In a large saucepan, heat 1 tablespoon (15 ml) of the olive oil over medium heat, add the couscous and stir to coat with the oil. Toast for about 2 minutes, until golden brown.

Add the water, cover and bring to a boil. Cook for about 6 minutes, or until the water has evaporated and the couscous is cooked through.

While the couscous is cooking, combine cranberries, capers and half of the scallions with the remaining 1 tablespoon (15 ml) olive oil and set aside. Once the couscous is cooked, turn off the heat, add the cranberry mixture and steam for about 2 minutes using the residual heat.

Season to taste with salt, add more capers if you desire and serve immediately, topped with the remaining scallions.

TIPS: Swapping raisins for the cranberries would also be delicious.

This recipe is also tasty chilled—just make ahead and refrigerate, then toss with extra olive oil right before serving. Once refrigerated, the couscous can stick together.

SWEET PUMPKIN CORNBREAD

Making cornbread from scratch is almost as easy as opening the boxed variety and doctoring it. If you are unsure about your baking skills, give this recipe a try—it really is that simple! This cornbread is sweet and delicious. It would be great served with my BBQ tofu grain bowl (page 119). I love mine warm, fresh out of the oven, with extra butter or honey (and I doubt anyone would make too much of a fuss if you mixed some honey into softened butter to make your own honey butter).

SERVES 8 TO 12

1 cup (157 g) finely ground cornmeal

1 cup (125 g) all-purpose flour

2 tsp (9 g) baking powder

½ tsp salt

1 tsp ground cinnamon

¾ cup (151 g) granulated sugar

⅓ cup (80 ml) melted butter

1 cup (245 g) pure pumpkin

¼ cup (60 ml) maple syrup

½ cup (120 ml) whole milk

2 large eggs

2 tbsp (15 g) coarse cornmeal

Preheat the oven to 375°F (190°C). Grease an 8 x 8-inch (20 x 20-cm) nonstick baking pan.

In a medium-size mixing bowl, combine the finely ground cornmeal, flour, baking powder, salt, cinnamon and sugar.

In a large mixing bowl, whisk together the butter, pumpkin, maple syrup, milk and eggs until well incorporated. Gradually add the dry ingredients, and whisk to combine.

Pour the batter into the baking pan and sprinkle the top with the coarse cornmeal.

Bake for 30 minutes, or until golden brown and a paring knife inserted into the center comes out clean.

TIP: Save yourself time by using 100% canned pure pumpkin. Pure pumpkin is unsweetened and contains only pumpkin, while pumpkin purée is sweetened and spiced.

PEANUT CHOCOLATE CHIP OATMEAL COOKIES

Traditional oatmeal cookies are loaded with plump raisins. But my version is packed with peanuts and chocolate chips—as if that could be bad, right? This recipe uses whole-wheat flour for a bit of a healthier base to make up for some of the less-than healthy mix-ins. These cookies came to be when I wasn't in the mood for a traditional oatmeal raisin cookie and wanted to make something sweet for my sister (who loves roasted peanuts)—she loved them, and I've kept making them ever since!

MAKES 12 COOKIES

---

1 ¾ cups (142 g) old-fashioned rolled oats

¾ cup (94 g) whole-wheat flour

2 tsp (2 g) ground cinnamon

½ tsp baking soda

¼ tsp salt

½ cup (112 g) salted butter, at room temperature

1 cup (230 g) packed brown sugar

1 tbsp (15 ml) vanilla extract

1 egg

½ cup (84 g) chocolate chips

½ cup (73 g) salted and roasted or honey-roasted peanuts

Preheat the oven to 350°F (180°C). Grease 2 parchment paper or aluminum foil–lined baking sheets.

In a medium-size bowl, combine the oats, flour, cinnamon, baking soda and salt.

In a stand mixer, blend the butter, brown sugar, vanilla and egg until well combined and light in color, about 5 minutes.

Add the dry mixture to the wet in 3 batches and turn the mixer on low to combine.

Once all of the dry ingredients are incorporated, add the chocolate chips and peanuts and stir by hand. Cover the dough and refrigerate for at least 30 minutes.

Using an ice cream scoop, form dough balls and place 6 on each baking sheet. Bake for 13 to 15 minutes, then let cool and serve. The cookies will harden as they cool.

TIP: If you are short on time, place the dough in the freezer to cool for about 15 minutes.

TOASTED ISRAELI COUSCOUS WITH OLIVES AND HAZELNUTS

Because of its size, flavor and texture, Israeli couscous is an interesting substitute for other grains such as rice, farro or barley. I especially like toasting it to get as much flavor as possible out of this round grain. Olives impart such a deliciously salty, briny, umami flavor to grain salads and many other dishes. I love the combination of olives, hazelnuts and lemon juice paired with the silky toasted Israeli couscous.

SERVES 4

2 tbsp (30 ml) olive oil, divided

2 cups (300 g) Israeli couscous

2 ½ cups (600 ml) water

½ cup (67 g) chopped mixed pitted olives

½ cup (56 g) hazelnuts

Juice of 1 lemon

Salt to taste

In a large saucepan, heat 1 tablespoon (15 ml) of the olive oil over medium heat, add the couscous and stir to coat with the oil. Toast for about 2 minutes, until golden brown.

Add the water, cover and bring to a boil. Let it cook for about 6 minutes, or until the water has evaporated and the couscous is cooked through. Turn off the heat, add the chopped olives and steam for about 2 minutes with the residual heat.

Meanwhile, toast the hazelnuts in a separate pan over medium-low heat until toasted and fragrant, about 2 minutes.

Add half of the hazelnuts to the couscous mixture and toss with the remaining 1 tablespoon (15 ml) olive oil and the lemon juice.

Season to taste with salt, then serve warm with the remaining hazelnuts sprinkled on top.

TIPS: I like using green and black olives for more color and variety, but use whatever you prefer.

Olives are salty, so be sure to taste the dish before you salt it—you can always add more salt if you need it.

ISRAELI COUSCOUS WITH MOZZARELLA AND PEPPADEWS

As I've mentioned, sweet and salty combinations are some of my favorites, and the pickled punch of the ever-so-slightly spicy peppadew peppers really intensifies the flavors of this dish. Ciliegine mozzarella are grape-size, fresh mozzarella balls, but any bite-size cheese will do. You could also dice a larger block of cheese if you can't find bite-size options. If you're feeling ultra ambitious, stuffing the peppadew peppers with the Ciliegine mozzarella would give this dish a totally different look.

SERVES 4

---

2 tbsp (30 ml) olive oil, divided

2 cups (300 g) Israeli couscous

2 ½ cups (600 ml) water

½ cup (72 g) peas

½ cup (90 g) white navy beans

½ cup (92 g) drained and quartered pickled mild peppadew peppers

½ cup (66 g) Ciliegine mozzarella

Salt to taste

In a large saucepan, heat 1 tablespoon (15 ml) of the olive oil over medium heat, add the couscous and stir to coat with the oil. Toast for about 2 minutes, until golden brown.

Add the water, cover and bring to a boil. Let cook for about 6 minutes, or until the water has evaporated and the couscous is cooked through. Turn off the heat, add the peas and steam for about 2 minutes with the residual heat, then set aside to cool.

In a large bowl, combine the white beans, peppadews and mozzarella cheese. Add the cooled couscous mixture and the remaining 1 tablespoon (15 ml) olive oil, then toss to combine. Season to taste with salt and serve.

> TIP: The seeds of the peppers are the hottest part, so if you are especially sensitive to spice, remove the seeds before tossing the peppers with the couscous.

CINNAMON SPICE VANILLA RICE PUDDING

Rice doesn't always have to be savory—it works nicely when sweet, too. I've always loved rice pudding, but growing up, it was never something that made it onto the menu. But now that I plan our menus, it's a special treat, though it's so easy to make that it really could be served all the time. Pumpkin adds a nice earthy and subtly sweet taste to so many dishes, and rice pudding is no exception!

SERVES 4

1 ¼ cups (300 ml) whole milk

¾ cup (180 ml) water

½ cup (93 g) medium-grain rice

1 tsp ground cinnamon, plus more for garnish

½ tsp ground nutmeg

⅓ cup (70 g) sugar

½ cup (120 g) pure pumpkin

1 large egg

2 tsp (10 ml) vanilla extract

⅛ tsp salt

Dried fruit (optional)

Chopped nuts (optional)

Chocolate chips (optional)

Combine the milk, water, rice, cinnamon and nutmeg in a pot and bring to a boil, stirring the mixture often. Reduce the heat to the lowest setting, cover and cook until the rice is soft and most of the liquid has evaporated, 20 to 25 minutes.

In a bowl, whisk together the sugar, pumpkin, egg, vanilla and salt until well combined. After 20 minutes of cooking the rice, remove it from the heat, add the sugar mixture and stir well to combine. Return to the heat and cook for 10 to 15 minutes longer. The longer you cook the rice, the thicker it will become.

Serve warm topped with extra cinnamon and anything you like: dried fruit, chopped nuts or chocolate chips.

ACKNOWLEDGMENTS

I would like to begin by thanking my husband, Stewart. You are the best friend, husband and editor I could ever ask for. Thank you for (almost!) always loving the food I serve you, and forever being my taste tester. You are truly one of a kind, and I'm so lucky to have you!

Thank you to my parents, Selma and Tom, who cheered me on while I was writing this book and celebrate all of my personal and professional successes as if they were their own. You are both great cooks (and eaters!), and I'm fortunate for your love and guidance.

Thank you to my sister, Erica, for helping me craft and brainstorm so many of my business ideas and creative content. You are incredibly smart and talented. I hope you love cooking from this book.

Thank you to my aunt, Nancy. Who is as good as you? You enthusiastically tried so many of these recipes—and inspired my love of photography.

Thank you to my dear friends, Tara and Tom, for your light and your boomerang—quite literally. Who would have thought in all of New York City we would live across the street from each other? You two are amazing friends and neighbors. I'm so grateful for your generosity and your friendship.

Thank you to Page Street Publishing for the amazing opportunity to author my first cookbook; what a joy it's been to write. Spending hours (and hours, and hours!) in the kitchen has felt like anything but work. I savored every minute of it.

ABOUT THE AUTHOR

Megan Wolf is a New York City–based registered dietitian, nutrition and wellness consultant and the owner of Megan Wolf Nutrition, a nutrition counseling and consulting private practice. She holds a master's degree in clinical nutrition from New York University. She lives (and cooks!) with her husband and daughter in New York City. She writes for her personal blog, The Domesticated Wolf, at www.thedomesticatedwolf.com. Megan's food philosophy is simple: Eat better, feel better, live better. She believes there's room in everyone's diet for all favorite foods, including a healthy dose of greens and grains. You can follow her for more health and recipe inspiration on Twitter @meganwolfrd, Instagram @thedomesticatedwolf and Facebook at The Domesticated Wolf.

INDEX